the Art of
LEADERSHIP

PROMOTING
EARLY CHILDHOOD SERVICES

Exchange Press

17725 NE 65th Street • B-275

Redmond, WA 98052

(800) 221-2864 • www.ChildCareExchange.com

THE ART of LEADERSHIP

Promoting Early Childhood Services

The Art of Leadership series replaces the popular Exchange Press textbook, *The Art of Leadership: Managing Early Childhood Organizations.* The entire series demonstrates the great complexity of an early childhood leader's job. Each volume expresses the importance of one aspect of this role. Each leader will need to prioritize all these roles based on many factors, including the skills that reside within the members of his team.

These articles were originally published in *Exchange Magazine.*
Every attempt has been made to update information on authors and other contributors
to these articles. We apologize for any biographical information that is not current.
Exchange is a bimonthly management magazine for directors, owners, and teachers
of early childhood programs. For more information about
Exchange and other Exchange Press publications for directors and teachers, contact:

Exchange Press
17725 NE 65th Street • B-275
Redmond, WA 98052
(800) 221-2864 • www.ChildCareExchange.com

ISBN 978-0-942702-61-3

Printed in Korea by Four Colour Print Group, Louisville, Kentucky

© Exchange Press, 2016

Cover Design: Scott Bilstad

the Art of
LEADERSHIP

PROMOTING
EARLY CHILDHOOD SERVICES

Introduction

Chapter 1: The Economics of Early Care and Education

Chapter 2: Advocating for Children and Families

Chapter 3: Promoting Your Program

Standing Up and Being Heard

The Director's Other Job

by Roger Neugebauer

"I spend half my time comforting the afflicted, and the other half afflicting the comfortable."

Wess Stafford

As President Emeritus of Compassion International, Wess Stafford has been a high-profile advocate for children in poverty worldwide. His work on a global scale mimics your work in leading an early childhood program on a local stage. You employ and motivate great teachers, you craft and maintain an engaging curriculum, and you support the parents in your program to be the best parents possible. But to really make a difference, your work must also be outwardly directed — seeking support needed to sustain your program as well as advocating for public policies that promote the well-being of all families.

This outward focus includes six key responsibilities.

1

Building Your Program's Reputation

Reputation is not just an ego thing. The reputation of your center has a direct impact on your ability to survive. An early childhood program with a great reputation will attract parents to enroll their children; a center with a poor reputation will find it difficult to get prospects in the door. A center with a great reputation will attract the best teaching candidates; a center with a poor reputation will have to make do with mediocre-to-poor candidates. A center with a great reputation will be on the radar of public agencies looking to place children, local employers seeking for a good place for their employees' children, and private funders desiring to support quality options for children; a center with a poor reputation will be avoided by those intending to promote quality services.

Building a great reputation in your community starts with providing great services. All the marketing in the world will not sustain a reputation if the services your program provides are not top notch. A high-quality program is one in which…

- children are being engaged and respected, where they are growing and learning and having fun.

- staff are challenged to develop their skills, work well together, enjoy themselves, and derive satisfaction from their work with children and parents.

- parents can trust that their children are in good hands, are kept informed on the progress of their children, and are greeted at the end of every day with joyful children.

Once your program is operating at a high level, don't let it be the best kept secret in town. Toot your horn. Your best marketing tool is word-of-mouth from contented parents — stimulate their word-of-mouth by telling them how important their sharing in the community is. Use social media tools to tell your story. Lure the press in with some catchy stories. Invite public officials, local instructors, local employers, and politicians in to visit your program (complete with the press on hand to capture their visits).

2
Maintaining High Enrollment

One of the keys to maintaining high quality in a program is ensuring enrollment is always maximized enough to balance the budget. You can be the best program in town, but if your enrollment lags you will need to start cutting corners and chipping away at what makes you special.

As noted above, running a stellar program with a high reputation is important. But it is not enough. You need your parents and teachers to be part of your marketing team recommending your program to parents in your community. Word-of-mouth is still the number one way parents find child care.

As today's young families are less attuned to newspaper and yellow page ads, you need to have a strong presence in cyberspace — you need an inviting, easy-to-navigate web presence. In addition, encouraging your teachers to share (anonymous) stories on a site like Facebook, can reach potential customers.

In addition, it's a good idea to find out where parents in your community go when searching for child care. As noted above, most parents talk to other parents for recommendations. But where else do they go for advice: to pediatricians, resource and referral agencies, health departments? When you determine where they go, make sure your program has a presence there — on their referral lists, flyers in their waiting areas, and champions everywhere.

Finally, if your program serves diverse populations, it's important to maintain a positive relationship with state and local agencies that support low-income families with public subsidies. Bureaucrats are people and often seek the path of least resistance, counting on dependable programs to serve the families they are supporting.

3
Securing Outside Resources

Unless your program is in an affluent suburb, you need more than parent fees to provide a high-quality program. Research has shown that nearly all programs rated at the highest quality have outside support — be it public funding, foundation funding, successful fundraising, or employer support.

This need for outside resources applies to both for-profit and non-profit programs. For-profit programs, while not eligible for some foundation funding, can solicit support from businesses and can conduct fundraisers. And, in a growing number of jurisdictions, for-profit programs are also eligible to serve families with public subsidies.

On the other hand, non-profit programs need not restrict their search for resources to traditional non-profit fundraising. In fact, many traditional approaches — seeking grants and holding fundraisers, while providing a temporary boost — may not build long-term sustainability. Making a deal with a major local employer to provide spaces for their employees may be more self-sustaining.

4
Uniting the Early Childhood Profession

In advocating for sound public policies, the biggest challenge in the early childhood world is that our profession is composed of several hundred thousand centers and homes. Pulling together a unified voice among this conglomeration of programs is a major challenge. Public schools, on the other hand, are organized into huge school districts, which can unite much more easily to promote common interests.

So one duty of an early childhood leader wanting to make a difference is to help create a profession out of the huge but diverse and very independent mix of players.

This work starts inside your own program where you need to help all your employees see themselves as part of an extremely important profession. Encourage or maybe support them in joining professional associations and participating in their workshops and conferences. Talk about local, state, and national news developments in early childhood initiatives and in staff meetings.

Then as you mature as a leader, take responsibility for growing and maintaining state and national associations. Volunteer to serve on committees, run for boards, and support policy initiatives.

5
Educating the Public about the Early Years

This past decade has seen a proliferation of good news about the importance of the early years and about the value of high-quality early care and education. Although those of us in the profession are well aware of this news, it's a noisy world. Parents, employers, and politicians who should hear these exciting messages are easily distracted by the latest disaster news, political craziness, or the updates on celebrities.

Early childhood leaders need to seek out opportunities to speak about the good news surrounding early years in public forums, private meetings with politicians and employers, in churches, at PTA meetings, and in political campaigns.

When you run across news stories, share them with all your parents and teachers and ask them to share, share, share. Post these stories on your social media sites. When politicians or editors promote incorrect information about the early years, write letters to the editor. Be the Johnny Appleseed of early care and education.

6
Advocating for Sound Public Policies

Last, and far from least, you need to be part of the advocacy team making sure that public policies support the needs of all families — families with high incomes as well as families struggling with multiple challenges. Everything you have done to accomplish the first five responsibilities listed above compounds to make you an effective advocate.

Your first task as an advocate is awareness. Note current funding and licensing policies that may have a negative bearing on the quality of your services. Keep on top of new legislation in the works that will impact the quality and quantity of services for children and families.

Next, find out where to exert influence to change, improve, or support policies and legislation. For example, if the way enrollment is calculated makes it impossible for you to provide continuity of care, provide specific examples of the unintended consequences of these policies to the key decisionmakers. If the state is considering passing a public school preschool initiative, which will remove four- and five-year-olds from community programs, don't wait to complain about it until after it is passed. Work your way on to committees planning the legislation, and attend and be vocal at public hearings about the legislation.

No One Said this Job Would be Easy

The Wess Staffords of the world did not get into positions of influence by taking the easy path. Being an effective early childhood leader is like having two full-time jobs — working inside to craft a program you and your staff can be proud of; and working outside to make sure the world knows what a good job you are doing and why all children and families deserve this standard of care. The good news is that this can happen — the world is filled with fantastic early childhood leaders who are making a difference… and enjoying what they are doing.

Roger Neugebauer

Roger Neugebauer is founding publisher of *Exchange* magazine and co-founder of the World Forum Foundation.

the Art of
LEADERSHIP

PROMOTING
EARLY CHILDHOOD SERVICES

1

CHAPTER 1

The Economics of
Early Care and Education

Prolonged Financial Malnutrition

by George Philipp

It is an amazing time to be in the early education field. In every state and community we see new funding opportunities and innovative approaches to supporting young children. Public acceptance of the importance of the first few years of life continues to spread rapidly. But watching the dramatic evolution of our field over the last few decades, I find myself haunted by a fundamental question. On the surface, we seem to be making great progress. Public policy is catching up with the wealth of new research on child development. New initiatives and funding opportunities are cropping up all over the country. Yet despite this, our field still seems to be struggling. Why is that?

In my mind, historically and presently, one persistent core issue has prevented us from creating a high-quality system for all children. That issue is the fact that we have never received adequate funding to achieve our goals. And even when policy makers acknowledge that our field is currently underfunded, they fail to take into account the effects of decades of previous inadequate funding. My diagnosis: the early education field is suffering the effects of *prolonged financial malnutrition.*

A person suffering from prolonged malnutrition would exhibit the following symptoms: constant hunger, weakness, confusion, stress, depression, and desperation. Analogously, these are all conditions that plague our field. And just as a person suffering from prolonged malnutrition needs to be put on a long-term recovery plan, so, too, our field needs a long-term, comprehensive solution that will allow us to recover from decades of poor funding.

Generally, there are two key things you need to do to be healthy: 1) eat a well-balanced and appropriate diet, and 2) get plenty of exercise. As we think of a healthy, high-quality early education workforce, we should start with a healthy diet that includes:

■ good compensation.

■ appropriate education/training.

■ a supportive work environment.

In conjunction with this, we need a regular exercise program that includes:

■ an appropriate amount of time for planning and reflection.

■ opportunities and support to transfer theory into practice.

■ peer-to-peer learning.

In this article I will examine each of these components in relation to the current realities of our field, building the case for how prolonged financial malnutrition has impeded our progress as a field and our intended outcomes for children and families.

Let's begin with protein. Without adequate protein, we simply cannot function well. And let's think about compensation as the protein in our diet. Early education funding has never addressed the poor compensation and working conditions facing people in our field. Even though protein is a critical component to a healthy diet, we have not supplied it to our field in a systematic and dependable way.

There are some great support programs out there like T.E.A.C.H. that provide stipends and reimbursement to support early educators. These programs are like a protein bar that provides some critical sustenance, but only temporarily alleviates real hunger. These types of programs are great to keep our energy up between meals, but should not be considered a replacement.

As we know, inadequate compensation doesn't just affect individuals in our field. Through high turnover and a limited ability to recruit talented staff, it also degrades the stability of our field as a whole. In the words of the recently released *Worthy work, STILL unlivable wages: The early childhood workforce 25 years after the National Child Care Staffing Study*, we need "to identify and mobilize a sustainable, dedicated source of public funding to upgrade the compensation of those who care for and educate our nation's young children."[1]

Now let's think about exercise. A good exercise program for our field would allow early educators the time and support they need to be exceptional teachers. This is another area where our current efforts fall short. Many current initiatives include some funds to provide staff release time, but these are usually short-term options that require programs to twist and contort their schedules to free up staff. Exercise shouldn't be something we are constantly trying to squeeze into our schedule. It should be a

regular component, like free play or staff meetings. We don't need a source of limited funding to free up a few staff to reflect on their recent training. We need stable funding to hire permanent additional staff so everyone gets the reflection and planning time they need. Policy makers need to understand that if you suffer from severe malnutrition it takes a long time to get healthy again. You need to start slow, eat a carefully monitored diet, and gradually enhance your exercise to increase strength and stamina. The reality of our field today is that intermittent, short-term support doesn't allow us to improve our daily practice in an intentional way over time. Interventions are often so sporadic that during the long breaks from one to the next, we lose momentum and cannot make the connections that would allow us to scaffold our professional development experiences.

One of the dangers our field currently faces is that we are imposing rapidly increasing expectations for what teachers should know and be able to do, without providing the necessary support and time to adapt to these heightened expectations. Think about athletes preparing for a marathon. They take their time building up their endurance and eat a carefully developed diet to support their workouts. Now think of a malnourished, out-of-shape person who trains and eats well for a week and then tries to run a marathon. Isn't that what we're doing in our current system — running a marathon when we are in no condition to do so?

Many of the quality improvement initiatives try to satiate us with certain types of food that will supposedly make us healthy overnight. We get a plate of 'superfoods,' but no main course and not enough time for adequate digestion. Sure, these limited meals may alleviate our current pangs of hunger and sustain us for short periods of time, but without a main course are we really going to get healthy? Nutritionists always talk about the importance of a balanced diet that includes the variety of foods our bodies need. They don't say that you can substitute more carbohydrates if you don't have any protein available.

Financial malnutrition is not just about being hungry and needing a good meal, it also affects our mood and how we behave. It makes us feel desperate, which leads to poor decision-making and engaging in activities that only provide short-term relief without long-term benefits. Yes, a great training series with follow-up coaching and reflection time can improve a teacher's practice, but it is not enough to create systemic change. We feel good because we got a healthy meal and a chance to exercise, but this effect is temporary and doesn't get us on a path to long-term health. Just as good nutrition requires a steady and consistent plan of healthy eating, high-quality programs require adequate compensation and integrated time for planning and reflection.

The desperation caused by financial malnutrition also leads us to accept things that we know are not good for our health. Like the empty calories in soda and candy bars, we invest precious time and money on trainings and projects that have no real impact on our skills or competencies. You know the feeling of sitting in a training and thinking to yourself, "Really, this is what I spent my money and time on?" Even worse, you know what it's like to participate in a useless activity because it is a requirement of a larger initiative in which your program is involved. When staff give up their valuable personal time in these situations, it takes a toll on their already poor state of health.

The long-term effects of our malnutrition have made us complacent and we have become accustomed to accepting whatever is offered. What we need to do is demand better. Not just better trainings; better infrastructure that creates a stable, healthy diet and exercise program. You know what happens when you eat junk food all the time? You get addicted to the short-term effects and disregard your long-term health. Do you know what happens when you are on a healthy diet for a long time? You lose your appetite for junk food.

In our field today, no one feels the pain of financial malnutrition more than directors. They are responsible for our programs and have to make the tough decisions on how to utilize limited funding to support their program and staff. They live under the constant stress of not being able to provide what is needed due to lack of funds. Think of a low-income parent who is hungry and has a family to feed. What do many low-income families end up buying at the grocery store? They look for what they can afford and provides the most meals; they don't have the luxury of buying the healthiest foods. They cannot afford the high cost of fresh meat, fruits, and vegetables. Directors deal with a similar challenge every day.

In addition, directors have to bear the burdens that come with quality initiatives just to squeeze out some extra support for their site. They spend their precious time completing data requests, having their site assessed, attending implementation meetings, and monitoring their staff to make sure they are complying with requirements. So again, you have a malnourished person being asked to do more exercise without the food they need, which only adds to their stress and poor overall health — not to mention those directors who need to manage multiple funding streams, each with their own requirements. Using the low-income parent analogy, these directors have to travel from store to store to pick up a few items at each, or work two or three jobs just to earn a little more money. Directors do all of this extra work to obtain subsidized funding for their families. Funding that doesn't usually meet the true cost of care. This sacrifice costs them valuable time they could be spending on their own health and the health of their staff.

It is not just people in our field who suffer from prolonged financial malnutrition. All of the organizations that support our programs suffer from it as well. In this arena the effects of malnutrition are even more pronounced. Organizations compete for limited funding, get very territorial, and often fight with one another. A common side effect of competing for funding is raising the expectations for what can be achieved. These high expectations are then passed on to the programs that participate. Wouldn't it be refreshing if all of the funders and initiatives out there said, "Wait a minute, first we are going to address compensation and staff needs to get the entire field at a basic level of good health, and then we can start intensive training and raise expectations." Instead, they try a quick fix to quality issues through some new approach to training and support. These initiatives would be a great way to support a healthy early education system. The problem is our current system is not healthy. It makes me think of all the quick-fix fad diets and programs like PX90 that claim you can lose weight and have a completely 'ripped' body in 90 days. It just doesn't work; and it wastes precious time and money because we are not starting at a place where they can be effective.

The responsibility for getting our field healthy does not rest solely on policy makers. We need to actively work to improve the situation. Imagine if someone gave you a subscription to a service that provided you with healthy food and a gym membership. You still have to eat the food and go to the gym to get healthy. Even if you don't get everything you need, there are always small lifestyle changes that you can make that add up to big differences. In our field today, we see many inspirational programs that do incredible things under the most challenging of funding circumstances.

I have painted a pretty grim picture of our field in this article, but if we are going to get healthy we need to be very clear about what is really holding us back. This article highlights a few areas of our field that are impacted by financial malnutrition. Coaches, trainers, higher education programs, and other areas also suffer from inadequate funding. We need to stop accepting short-term efforts that do not support the long-term health of our field — and also stop accepting that a large-scale sustainable funding stream to improve compensation and support is not viable.

There are programs, communities, and states that are making great progress towards better health. Why? Because they follow the basic ideas behind good health, understand that it will take a long time to create the system they want, and are creating stable, long-term funding streams to reach their goals. At one point in our history, our country made a criti-cal decision to invest in public education. Now we need the same level of large scale, sustainable investment in our early education system. We need to take a stand and be clear that we are on a long road of recovery to reach the ultimate goal of providing high-quality programs for all children. Taking a page from basic child development theory, kids must first and foremost be healthy, feel safe, and have the time to explore and learn in a high-quality environment. Shouldn't we insist on the same basic foundation for early educators?

Endnotes

1 Whitebook, M., Phillips, D., & Howes, C. (2014). *Worthy work, STILL unlivable wages: The early childhood workforce 25 years after the National Child Care Staffing Study.* Berkeley: Center for the Study of Child Care Employment, University of California, Berkeley.

George Philipp

George Philipp is a Senior Program Associate for the WestEd E3 Institute located in San Jose, California. He leads early educator professional development initiatives locally, regionally, and state-wide through E3 Institute's workforce development initiatives. George is the proud father of two young children who teach him how precious life is every day. He can be reached at gphilip@wested.org.

The author offers thanks to:
Randi Wolfe, Marcy Whitebook, Rory Darrah,
John Gunnarson, Lea Austin, and his wife, Tania,
whose mentoring, support, and friendship
have kept him passionate about the work he does
and made this article possible.

Creating Political Will

Reframing Our Position on the Value of ECE

by Sherry M. Cleary

Most Early Childhood Education professionals can't understand why the rest of the country is not passionately supportive of our work. We each know the value of our service — to the children we work with, their families, the economy, and society. It seems so obvious! Children who experience a nurturing, rich, and stimulating early childhood experience have a much better chance of realizing a healthy productive life. It takes a village to raise a child and early childhood programs known for their excellence become the extended family providing the traditional support that is known to ensure healthy development. And families who have reliable, high-quality early childhood services for their children can work — AND their work is better. These families work more productively, have better attendance, and even steal less from their employers! Parents who are students, in either high school or college, do better academically and graduate in a more timely fashion when they have high-quality early childhood services for their young children. Society is better off for the high-quality programs available. Over the years several longitudinal studies have been published that demonstrate the long-term benefits — the return on investment — of high-quality early childhood programs. Young children who have a great start seem to be more successful throughout life: they graduate from high school, go on to college, are better

employed, pay taxes, and are healthier than their peers who didn't have access to excellence.

All of this good news ought to generate huge investments for early childhood education. And while we have seen a significant increase in funds from both federal and local sources in the last six years, the field continues to struggle. Some of the federal funds are about to dry up with states worried about how to sustain their gains. And the federal government is considering landmark changes in the funding models of early childhood, but we wonder will there be political will to enact these changes? What does it take to create political will? In the last two years the appreciation of early childhood education has increased notably . . . it polls well with both Democrats and Republicans. The newest batch of candidates is likely to include early childhood as one of their platform issues. But why doesn't the funding of early childhood education come more easily?

We might be more successful if, instead of talking about the long-term return on investment that excellent well-funded early childhood education yields, we talk about the *short-term return on investment*. Some individuals don't have the patience for long-term returns . . . sometimes we have to focus on the good that gets generated when we do the right thing

NOW. When children are taught by well-educated and trained teachers who bring their creative energy and passion to the early childhood classroom, we see all children having a much stronger chance to meet the challenges immediately ahead. Children manage social and emotionally-charged situations with greater agency. They are known to persevere and bring problem-solving skills to their work. They learn how to advocate for each other. Their innate curiosity has been nurtured and they perceive themselves as learners.

Additionally, we know that the immediate effect that high-quality early childhood programs have on parents is of essential value. Anyone who has ever parented a child knows how challenging it can be. A well-designed and implemented early childhood program serves as the extended family for a person striving to do right by a young child. This is the case for young and inexperienced parents as well as it is for experienced parents, including grandparents who may find themselves with the task of raising their young grandchildren. In any of these cases, the early childhood program becomes an integral partner and supports the family unit — however it is defined. Strong programs provide guidance, support, and, if necessary, referrals to services found in the community. These programs, with their two-generation strategies, help to ensure the mental health and stability of families, as well as make sure that the adults can get to work and be productive. Do we — as a society — want families to live on unemployment insurance and/or public assistance or do we want to encourage gainful employment that builds a family's self-esteem and ensures a regular contribution to the community's tax base? The immediate return on the early childhood investment is evident and an essential piece of society's fabric. The value of these immediate impacts matter to our society and reduce costs that are often associated with families in high need.

Parents who want to pursue their education find that campus-based child care programs make significant contributions to their realization of goals. Oftentimes the early childhood programs help parents learn to navigate parenthood and the pursuit of higher education by providing guidance and expectations regarding the balance that is essential for success. The parent who enrolls a child in high-quality early childhood on or near campus has a higher rate of timely graduation. Retention rates of these student parents can be as high as 94% — a stark contrast to the larger student body statistics. Further, student parents who receive support during the process find and sustain employment, earn more than their peers, and raise children who have been exposed to a greater respect of education. These immediate returns on the investments of high-quality early childhood education make for very significant and compelling arguments to strengthen public and political will.

The short-term return on investment can also be calculated by the number of young children who are promoted successfully each year in school. Each time a school retains a child in a grade, the district expends a considerable amount of money. The increased costs are not limited to the additional year of education the district becomes responsible for, although that cost alone is considerable. Children who repeat a grade often suffer additional stigma and setbacks, which can increase the likelihood that they will be candidates for additional services and may be retained again later on. And in the United States, we know that children are held back in kindergarten and first grade. We know that this occurs more frequently when young children have not had the opportunity to experience excellence in early childhood education. The cost of grade retention in the early years is only one metric to consider.

We can and should calculate the impact that high-quality early childhood education has on the need for early intervention and special education services. There is ample anecdotal data to suggest that early childhood experiences have reduced or eliminated the need for subsequent special education services. High-quality early childhood experiences have a high incidence of mitigating the need for special education placements in primary school. In some instances the early childhood services that are paired are enough to reduce the need for subsequent special education services. In other cases, the integration of special provisions via early intervention services early in development can mean that a child needs less support later and over the long term. And in other circumstances, the child simply does much better when services begin earlier and child and family become accustomed to making the most of the services available. Again, the immediate savings is considerable and impressive.

These are just a few examples of the catalytic value that investments in high-quality early childhood yield in just a year or two. It may be time to help increase political will by illustrating that high-quality early childhood experiences create a significant short-term return on investment. Now is the time to invest well and recoup the rewards. Social science talks about the value of two-generation strategies. I think we have the perfect two-generation strategy, and it would be a shame to forget about the immediate return on our investments.

Sherry M. Cleary

Sherry M. Cleary is the Executive Director of the New York Early Childhood Professional Development Institute, which is housed at the City University of New York. She leads the work of a dynamic, intelligent, and passionate team dedicated to building essential systems to ensure a highly effective early childhood workforce for the state of New York, to guarantee that young children have access to excellence. Sherry co-chairs the Governor's Early Childhood Advisory Council for the state of New York. She is also the Past-President and President-Elect of the New York State Association of Early Childhood Teacher Educators (NYSAECTE). Last year, Sherry was named to Mayor de Blasio's six-member Early Childhood Working Group, initially charged with building the model to be used for a Universal Pre-Kindergarten implementation in New York City. Ms. Cleary has worked in the field of early childhood education as a classroom teacher, a program administrator, and as both a faculty member and higher education administrator for more than 35 years. She has deep experience in inner cities and rural communities. Sherry has served on several Boards of Directors and College Advisory Boards as well as presided over national and regional membership organizations.

Worthy Work with Continued Unlivable Wages

by Margie Carter

Reading the updated 2014 research report on the early childhood workforce, *Worthy Work, STILL Unlivable Wages* (Whitebook, Phillips, & Howes, 2014), both depressed and infuriated me. In case you missed it, the research highlights include these salient points:

■ Child care providers' wage growth was lower than the growth in wages paid to fast food workers. The mean hourly wage of a child care worker in 2013 was $10.33 an hour or $21,490 annually. This puts child care workers in the Bureau of Labor Statistics' lowest income tier along with parking lot attendants and dry cleaners, meaning that most child care workers live in poverty.

■ People providing early care and education to three- to- five-year-olds outside of a school setting earn two-thirds of what their peers earn in school-sponsored Pre-K, and half of what they earn in kindergarten. Those who seek out higher degrees still earn less than they would in another field. Pre-K teachers with a bachelor's degree make just three-quarters of what female college graduates make in the general workforce.

■ The combination of low wages and the rising cost of living means that many child care workers aren't paid enough to meet their families' most basic needs. In fact, more than 46% of child care workers are in families using one of the four major social support programs — almost double the rate of use in the U.S. workforce overall.

■ Nearly half of child care workers live in families that rely on one or more public programs, compared to a quarter of the overall workforce. Nearly three-quarters are worried about being able to pay their bills, while half are worried about being able to afford food for their families.

■ Child care workers who endure the stressors of living in poverty are more likely to experience toxic stress, depression, and chronic health issues. As the number of children spending time in child care settings has increased, so too has our knowledge of the link between adult caregiving and early childhood brain development. Study after study has shown the connection between better-paid staff and higher quality care. The instability and stress experienced by caregivers dealing with economic insecurity or poverty shapes their ability to provide enriching and nurturing environments for children. Often, it can result in a decreased ability to provide supportive spaces for children to develop and learn.

Perhaps it's a rhetorical question to ask how we find ourselves in this predicament. The importance of the first five years in a child's life is well documented, especially in light of ever more sophisticated neuro-science and how the human brain develops. Public discourse now endorses the need for universal Pre-Kindergarten programs while the early child-hood profession continues to amass an ever-grow-ing array of tools to measure and promote quality improvement. How, in this context, have we over-looked the urgency to upgrade compensation and viable working conditions for teachers in these set-tings? Despite evidence to the contrary, do we believe the lack of a livable wage won't impact the stability of the teaching workforce and thereby the quality of the program? Why have our professional initiatives and public dollars continued to burden teachers with more requirements, but failed to establish a parallel commitment to more pay and an infrastructure to ensure this as a viable profession for people to enter?

Among the many poignant comments at the confer-ence the New America organization held to highlight the *Worthy Work, STILL Unlivable Wages* report, those from Megan Gunnar, Director of the Institute of Child Development and Professor at the Uni-versity of Minnesota, really grabbed my attention. Known for her work on the committee that devel-oped *Neurons to Neighborhood* (Shonkoff & Phillips, 2000), Gunnar reminded the conference attendees that the complexity involved in nurturing the devel-opment of young children in group settings requires a level of executive functioning in teachers that is not possible under conditions of high stress. Perhaps Gunnar's point contributes to the growing use of the term 'teacher proofing' as an anecdote or substitute for addressing a significant source of that stress — their own poverty wages.

'Teacher proofing' implies it doesn't matter who the teacher is: teachers just do what they are told to do without having to think about it. How does this preposterous idea fit with the research highlighting the importance of a child's relationship with atten-tive, caring adults as central to the growth of his or her brain, emotional intelligence, and ongoing learn-ing into productive adulthood? If we give teachers a script to guide their curriculum, do we really believe this will reduce stress or lead to genuine relation-ships with the children?

While wages have not significantly improved since the first child care staffing study (Whitebook, Phillips & Howes, 2014), expectations and per-formance requirements have certainly increased, adding to the stress teachers already experience trying to manage their personal lives on inadequate salaries. Teachers want to do right by the children, take pride in meeting all the standards and scoring well on rating scales. More and more is required of them, while the delight of being with children is slipping away. The work remains worthy, but it is not sustainable.

Despite evidence to the contrary, do we believe the lack of a livable wage won't impact the stability of the teaching workforce and thereby the quality of the program?

An Interview with Angie Roberson and Rosemarie Vardell

So what happened to the Worthy Wage Movement that held such promise? How did it lose momen-tum and become replaced by quality rating systems that don't address compensation as an essential ingredient for a stable, qualified workforce? As I watched the newscast of the New America report, I was heartened to see Angie Roberson on one of the panels, someone I knew 15 years ago when she worked at the Center for the Childcare Workforce (CCW). I caught up with her in North Carolina where she, along with Rosemarie Vardell and a cadre of other dedicated folks, continue to address compensation issues in their state.

Margie: As you read the update on the child care staffing report, I'm curious about your reaction.

Angie: I was shocked to be honest. I thought we had made more progress in wages for our work-force. But when you look at wages over 25 years, it is just sad. I know part of the reason that wages have not gone up is because money was used to put rating systems in place as a strategy to increase the quality; but the work of teaching young children has gotten much harder, too (more regulations, more education requirements, helping children in crisis). I worked at a lab school for years and watched soon-to-be teachers excited about teaching young children, and it was wonderful for me to be in that environment. I also felt that it was my duty to be honest with the soon-to-be teachers about wages, because that is what my mentor (Rosemarie) did for me. Now I have to walk that fine line to not discourage them from teaching in child care but, instead, encourage them to seek the highest quality programs to work for and not settle for inadequate wages. We do the work of teaching because we love children, because we love to watch the process of learning 'when it clicks,' and because we love laughter and smiles. But we need to be able to afford to have families of our own, too, and not be in debt for the rest of our lives.

Rosemarie: In some ways it is unbelievable that our early childhood workforce is still being paid wages that in no way reflect the critical and complex nature of this work. This national report, along with our state level reports, provides such important tools for advocates as we educate decision-makers about the current reality of child care jobs. Today, we have social media as a tool for awareness and education, but we still have not answered the question of who will step up to make compensation the focus of organizing for necessary policy changes that will make higher wages possible.

Recent work with teachers in our community underlines their ability to express the urgency of improving compensation and the impact of continuing not to do so in a substantial, sustainable way. At our gatherings, teachers provide stories that call out the significance of providing children with foundational skills and experiences. One teacher described going to an emergency room and receiving excellent, compassionate care from a nurse who she had taught as a four-year-old. The teachers also identified a lack of political power and access to decision-making tables as barriers to making compensation an urgent

issue to be addressed. Since many teachers are raising families, going to school and working second (or third) jobs, they are short on energy and time to organize and advocate for change.

Margie: How true! To me, that fact should compel those of us in more privileged positions to bring these teachers' stories to the table, even as we work to get the teachers there in person to help shape the way forward.

Rosemarie: One of the questions still unanswered is: "Who will lead this effort to improve compensation?" Teachers still need 'facilitative leaders' or 'an organizational home' that will provide the capacity, resources, training, and support so that teachers can engage in efforts for fair pay and respect for their work.

Margie: Who will step up and provide this home? NAEYC and their affiliates? R&R organizations? QRIS state systems? What will it take for them to make this a top priority?

Will Educational Requirements Improve Compensation?

Margie: While we want all teachers and providers engaged in ongoing learning, how can they take on this financial and time burden in the context of their already stressed lives? And, what's the real incentive with these educational requirements when people can leave the field and get equal, if not better, pay doing something else? I'm struck that given the low wages we haven't see a robust scholarship, along with student loan forgiveness program for early childhood educators.

Angie: The teachers who I am working with through my current job have been able to access T.E.A.C.H. scholarships and some even have supports at their workplace to pay for classes along with release time to attend classes. I think until our field is viewed as a profession, we are not going to see the incentives across the board to encourage teachers to seek more education in a low-paying field. On the other hand, although there are not more incentives in place, I hear teachers talk about how more education changed the way they teach because they've gained a 'why' for what they do and gained more effective strategies for their toolbox.

Rosemarie: Adding to Angie's point, the T.E.A.C.H. Early Childhood® (T.E.A.C.H.) Initiative is active in 24 states and the District of Columbia. Through this scholarship effort, 15,622 early educators working in 8,289 early childhood programs have continued their education. With this support, providers and teachers are doing their part to attend college and earn degrees. However, while this has resulted in somewhat higher wages, they are not even close to wages of similarly educated members of the general labor force.

What Kind of Teacher Preparation Will Make a Difference?

Margie: Going back to Megan Gunnar's point about the complexities and stress of working in early childhood education, I'm concerned that teacher education or ongoing professional development experiences aren't really preparing teachers to be professionals, but, instead, lower-paid technicians. What learning experiences do career-oriented teachers need to strengthen their ability to negotiate all the expectations in light of their desire to address each child's competency and learning opportunities? So much of what is called teacher education or training today is focused on meeting requirements and delivering curriculum. Advocacy and leadership skills are not often part of their higher ed curricula. To counter the notion of 'teacher-proof curriculum,' Parker Palmer asserts that good teaching comes from "strengthening the identity and integrity of the teacher." To my mind, this notion should be central to our teacher education and ongoing professional development work. How do we advocate for teachers learning not just techniques, but critical thinking and reflective practices so they are genuinely able to

---

Working on Compensation Issues

Thoughts from Angie Roberson

- Start the conversation with teachers and providers; give them the data that we have and a way to understand it and share it.

- Talk with families as allies, not as the source to fix the problem.

- Talk with businesses to help them understand the role that the child care industry plays in their businesses and ways they can support our efforts.

- Encourage decision makers to spend time with the child care workforce in child care programs to see how crucial and valuable the work is.

---

do right by children and fulfill the meaning of their work?

Angie: I am concerned about these issues, too. I visited a program recently for transitional families (families new to the United States, learning English) and the teacher was so amazing. I remember saying, "There could have been crying children there all day, but she set the tone for safety, happiness, and making friends." Teachers have to sometimes take on the emotional pieces for their children and help them through it. I was changed as a teacher when I had to help a toddler deal with his mother dying. No one prepared me for that and how I felt or how he felt. I hope I did it right; I think I did. During and after that experience we were able to get the supports we needed, but not all programs can identify or afford the resources needed to support teachers. Teachers are not being prepared for the kinds of teaching situations that they have to take on. I think we could advocate for portions of education classes to be dedicated to critical thinking skills or more field experiences enabling teachers learn reflective practices.

We have started a peer mentoring project in our community to show teachers how to think about what they do and why that intentionality is so powerful. We see a change in their classrooms soon after their mentor starts working with them (and a change sometimes in the mentor's classroom, too, as he or she begins to understand more about reflective teaching practices through their conversations and work together).

A Call to Action

Margie: The data in the recent report on wages and teachers' lives is so powerful. I'm wondering what we can do at the community level to turn it into a call for action. We can't just wait and hope that someone else will deal with this. We now have even more data to press on our professional organizations to make this issue a priority and to urge them to create an organizational home for teacher efforts to gain better compensation and professional respect. What approach are you taking to address these issues in your work and what are you learning from your efforts?

Angie: We are taking data from this recent study and our local data and putting it in the hands of teachers, family child care providers, directors, and families to help them be articulate about the problem. We have to be clear about our messaging and goals. We are not asking for families to pay more for their children's care and education; rather, we are asking for a larger investment from communities and particularly businesses that benefit from child care programs whose services support their community of workers.

Rosemarie: Yes, we are focusing on strengthening grassroots leadership, including advocacy, and increasing teachers' knowledge of early childhood systems and how decisions are made about public funding. Teachers are getting stronger in describing their roles in quality early childhood education and communicating the compensation research to the public. These are crucial skills because the current political discourse does not tie how well children are being educated to teachers and their skills. This makes their role and economic plight invisible.

The Worthy Wage group in our county included a "90:1" campaign as part of its advocacy activities leading up to Worthy Wage Day, May 1, 2015. The "90" stands for the percentage increase in parent fees over the last 25 years, while the "1" stands for the increase in teacher wages in our state. Teachers and family child care providers completed postcards that were delivered to decision-makers in our community and our state legislature.

I'd like to add a final thought. In a recent gathering in our community where teachers met with college students to tell them about their low-wage work, I got a glimpse of another issue — the stigma of being poor. At first the teachers focused their comments on how rewarding the work is and said little about the wages. One teacher finally said, "I don't really want people to know I am poor. There is such a stigma attached to that." A sense of pride in their work keeps some teachers from wanting to get involved in grassroots work to address compensation. Teachers who have transformed a stigma into righteous indignation are showing all of us where to take this work.

References

Child Care Services Associates. (2015). T.E.A.C.H. Early Childhood National Center Fact Sheet. www.childcareservices.org/wp-content/uploads/2013/05/TEACH-Center_FactSheet_1_15v4.pdf

Palmer, P. (2007). *The courage to teach.* San Francisco: Jossey-Bass.

Shonkoff, J., & Phillips, D. (Eds.). (2000). *Neurons to neighborhoods: The science of early childhood development.* Washington DC: Committee on Integrating the Science of Early Childhood Development, Board on Youth and Families, National Academies Press.

Whitebook, M., Phillips, D., & Howes, C. (2014). *Worthy work, STILL unlivable wages: The early childhood workforce 25 years after the National Child Care Staffing Study.* Berkeley: Center for the Study of Child Care Employment, University of California, Berkeley.

Margie Carter

Margie Carter is the co-founder of Harvest Resources Associates (www.ecetrainers.com) and the co-author of numerous books and early childhood videos. As she moves towards retirement years, her professional work is focused on highlighting and supporting the inspiring work of new leaders and uplifting the voices and leadership of teachers in the field.

Angie Roberson

Angie Roberson received her bachelor's degree at the University of North Carolina at Greensboro where she has worked in a variety of child care programs as a toddler teacher. Her roles in the early childhood field have included being assistant director at a lab school, working for a national organization (Center for the Childcare Workforce), and coordinating all the training for More at Four. Currently, Angie is the coordinator of a new quality improvement project in Guilford County, EQuIPD (Education Quality Improvement and Professional Development). She is the mother of a middle schooler, former PTA president, and aspiring yogi.

Rosemarie Vardell

Rosemarie Vardell, Ph.D., has served on the planning committee, is the lead trainer, and will guide the work of the learning coach to support implementation of the series. She has worked in the field of Early Childhood Education for over 35 years. During this time her focus has been on leading quality early childhood programs; teaching, training and supporting the early childhood workforce to offer high-quality programs for all children; facilitating the development of teachers as leaders and mentors; making the connection between high-quality work environments and quality education for young children; advocating for fair and equitable state and federal policies that impact young children and families; and, facilitating the strengthening of cultural competence of the early childhood workforce though action-oriented learning and organizational improvements. Her professional experiences include university teaching, administering early childhood programs, training and workforce development in non-profit organizations, and early childhood program monitoring in a state agency. During her career she developed and implemented three workforce training programs, including Leadership Empowerment Action Project (LEAP), Taking on Turnover, and Model Work Standards. She trained a cadre of diverse trainers to effectively use these models and developed a national early childhood training institute, Leaders in Action. Dr. Vardell has developed and taught graduate and undergraduate courses for teachers on Early Childhood Leadership and Mentoring. She has published peer-reviewed articles, been awarded public and private grants, and been a presenter/facilitator at numerous state and national conferences.

ECE Meets Economics

The Changing World of Early Education and Care

by Gwen Morgan and Suzanne Helburn

Those of us identified with high-quality child care, early education, and family support (ECE) are experiencing new trends in our field that are interacting with old problems. We want to define our roles in the emerging system and influence policies that will affect us. Recently, economists have begun to recognize our importance, not just our benefits for poor children, but also our benefits to businesses, the economy, and society. This article will summarize our old problems and new trends, as we see them, and discuss how economists can help us develop a more effective ECE system in our states and communities.

Our Old and Continuing Problems

The Trilemma. The budget trilemma of quality, compensation, and affordability continues to afflict the field. The trilemma has to be understood as a system of interrelated problems. Otherwise, improving one of the three occurs at the expense of one of the others. Measures to increase quality reduce affordability and affect compensation.

Only a few providers solve the trilemma: those with access to enough funding to provide quality. The trilemma stems from grossly inadequate funding for ECE, what economists call inadequate effective demand: the fact that most buyers are not willing or able to pay for good quality services.

This inadequacy of effective demand shows up most prominently in the difficulty in finding and keeping highly skilled personnel, particularly people of color. Compensation is inadequate to attract and keep the quality of staff needed. Our inability to pay adequately has already resulted in a decline in the percentage of early childhood teachers and workers with degrees. During the same period, the number of colleges offering specialized early education and care degrees has also dropped (Herzenberg et al., 2005).

Multiple government-created single purpose programs and funding streams. Individual programs, each created to solve a specific problem, include programs for poor children, children of the military, children with special needs, and programs to reform welfare, to improve schools, to treat family problems, and to prevent crime and delinquency. None of them is adequately funded.

Three decades of single-problem programs have resulted in major unintended consequences: competition for funds, narrow definitions of what the service is, overlaps, a 'gap group' between the poor and the well-to-do, segregation of children by category, inadequate basic supply/demand data, lack of continuity of services, disparities in eligibility of families with the same needs and in compensation for staff with the same qualifications, disincentives for moving children out of poverty, inconsistent infrastructure.

Two Emerging Trends: Universal Pre-Kindergarten and State Quality Improvement Initiatives

Universal Pre-K as a trend is too new to determine whether it can be incorporated into a seamless mixed system of auspices, or is just one more competing 'program' adding to the problems in the system. School-based Pre-K is currently a very small part of the whole. Thirty-eight states now have at least one Pre-K classroom in at least one school. A few states — Arkansas, California, Florida, Georgia, Illinois, Massachusetts, New Jersey, New Mexico, New York, Oklahoma, and Wisconsin — are moving toward universally available Pre-K programs, usually for four-year-olds and mainly part-day. Only four states currently offer universal Pre-K, and even fewer of those appear to favor a mixed system.

Policy-makers are influenced by three often-quoted longitudinal studies of the effects of high-quality Pre-K programs on later success in school, college, jobs, communities, and family life. Long-term benefits to the economy of high-quality Pre-K, it is argued, will more than offset the cost of the programs. However, it is not generally understood that replicating these positive outcomes will necessitate incorporating the characteristics of the original three studies: starting early, employing more teachers with degrees in ECE, assuring intensive relationships with parents (Herzenberg et al., 2005).

A potential unintended consequence could be an actual decline in availability of services for infants, toddlers, and three-year-olds. If most four-year-olds were attracted to free services in schools, existing centers would lose enrollment. Some private pre-schools that have depended on fees from four-year-olds to help finance their total program could be

forced out of business, reducing the availability of ECE for still younger children.

State Quality Initiatives. In the past decade, states have developed initiatives to improve the quality of all ECE programs. When substantial federal dollars became available for quality improvement, leaders, officials, and advocates joined forces to develop new initiatives, often attracting private dollars for their efforts.

Many of the innovative ideas had already been developed before states had federal dollars to implement them. Since the early 1990s, groups of state agency staff and community advocates have been planning together to implement a more systemic approach to developing the early education and care workforce. These approaches began with creating a career lattice and coherent pathways to higher qualifications. By 2004, there were at least 40 such planning groups across the country, starting to implement strategies that were feasible in their locations. Tiered quality rating systems are one example of the new innovations.

Whatever their starting point, the career development planning groups in the states were led to other elements of the ECE system that needed to be changed. They went through a discovery process in which each change led to the next necessary piece. They implemented career lattices, personnel registries, core knowledge, T.E.A.C.H. scholarships, and many other improvements. These innovations were interconnected, and they helped connect infrastructure more broadly across the sectors.

Early Care and Education as a System

A system is a set of interdependent elements that together perform some function. The interdependence between parts means that a change in one element causes change in other parts of the system, and affects the performance of the whole system.

Lynn Kagan's formula for defining an ECE system is:
Programs + Infrastructure = System

Clifford and Gallagher have likened infrastructure to that which is essential to put a soldier into the battlefield. For our field, many elements of an adequate infrastructure already exist, at least in nascent form, e.g. Resource and Referral Agencies, state licensing bureaus, higher education, community and state-level planning groups or agencies created to implement a new function. Ordinarily, they are underfunded, and not connected as a system, so that their full potential has not been realized.

The piecemeal development of publicly-funded ECE programs has contributed to today's problems. We do not want new developments to further complicate the creation of an effective system of early care and education.

What Economists Can Contribute

Economists have been helpful in conceptualizing ECE as a market system and ECE provision as an industry. Even when their use of language is new to some of us, they are also powerful allies in justifying significant increases in public (and public/private) investments in ECE.

Subsidizing ECE Infrastructure. Most ECE services are purchased by parents or by government from private providers competing in a local market. Publicly financed (Head Start) and publicly operated programs (school-based Pre-K programs) is a smaller part of supply, but they definitely affect market conditions. Economists have argued that public support of infrastructure is necessary to improve market performance. Furthermore, they have estimated the cost of infrastructure investments.

Here is the argument: In the local child care market competition creates pressures to cut costs and keep fees just barely above costs, so that profit or surplus are low. The main way to cut costs is either to employ fewer workers or hire low-skill workers for low pay.

Because they operate on the margin, providers can't afford to pay for staff training.

Parents cannot easily monitor their child's care and often are inadequately informed about what constitutes good quality or what alternative services exist. This creates potential market imperfections, and parents can be sold lower quality services than they think they are buying.

To operate efficiently these markets need institutions to service and regulate the market. ECE market infrastructure services are needed — adequately-funded public regulation and enforcement, applied research and development, incentives to achieve higher levels of quality, resource and referral services for parents and providers, access to training programs tied to pathways to degree programs. However, because profit or surplus margins are so low, the infrastructure for ECE is not likely to develop without public support.

Subsidizing Direct Services. As economists see it, the big problem facing the ECE system is inadequate effective demand, the inability or unwillingness of parents to pay for enough high-quality services. Paying for child care and early education has traditionally been the responsibility of parents. Economists make a compelling argument for public investment in ECE based on the 'public good' aspect of ECE services that benefit society at large, not just the individual families. Parents will buy only the amount and quality of services they are willing to pay for to satisfy their family's needs. If we want to reap the benefits of ECE services for society as a whole, we must be willing to pay for them from the public purse.

To convince the public that the investment is worth making, economists compare the costs and benefits of a particular policy, quantifying the benefit per dollar invested. They estimate the long-run public benefits of ECE services in reducing public spending:

■ on education when fewer children are held back or require special education services.

- on the criminal justice system because fewer adolescents and adults get arrested.

- on public health because fewer teenagers have babies.

- on labor development when ECE helps individuals complete more schooling, so that they earn higher wages over their lifetimes, and pay more taxes.

In helping to develop more productive workers, ECE contributes to higher rates of economic growth for the society. Heckman and Masterov show that investment in ECE is a better bet in creating human capital (people's productivity on the job) than other interventions requiring public spending. They compare the benefits per dollar spent on ECE to the benefits from programs for adolescents or training programs for adults. They argue the earlier the intervention, the greater the long-run payoff for society (Heckman & Masterov, 2004).

Economists have also estimated the short-run impact of ECE in promoting economic growth in a region. These impact studies use the same approach used to justify building a football stadium or some other publicly-funded project. They estimate how much additional income is generated for the region from the ECE industry. The added income comes from the ability of parents to hold a job, and the additional local spending generated by ECE providers in supplying their services. Economists have also estimated how much spending is needed, how much business and philanthropy can help, and who should get the subsidies — parents or providers. Helburn and Bergmann recommend public subsidies for infrastructure and vouchers so that no parent pays more for ECE than 20% of their above-poverty level income (Helburn, 2002). David Blau (2001) advocates direct dollar payments to parents to use either to care for their own children or to purchase ECE services. In contrast, ECE advocates tend to favor subsidies to providers. Economists point out that such subsidies tend to distort fees so that they do not reflect costs, and therefore quality, weakening an important market signal of quality.

Conclusions

ECE will probably continue to be dominated by privately provided care even though public school participation will increase. Government will probably continue to use purchase-of-service methods of subsidy, which shore up effective demand. Universal Pre-K may be another 'program' potentially at odds with a systems approach. Some states, however, are creating an infrastructure at the same time they are developing or expanding Pre-K. In taking a more integrated approach to infrastructure, they may be able to align the different funding programs to reduce the unintended consequences that the ECE world has known.

Adequate staff compensation to attract and retain well-educated personnel remains a major hurdle to be overcome. Public schools are more likely to pay ECE teachers at levels comparable to that of elementary school teachers. Unions may become allies in public schools and the Head Start sector. With the advent of quality rating systems, parents may demand and some will be able to pay for higher quality. But a substantial influx of dollars is needed to create the demand for high-quality services. The federal government has the greatest ability to create large and needed funding for a system. However, currently, state politicians are more aware of the public good aspect of ECE, and states are the appropriate public entities to manage evolving ECE systems. Our challenge is to work together to build the public will that will make ECE public funding a priority, and to build a system that can help ECE markets function effectively.

References

Blau, D. (2001). *The child care problem: An economic analysis.* New York: Russell Sage Foundation.

Helburn, S., & Bergmann, B. (2002). *America's child care problem: The way out.* New York: Palgrave for St. Martin's Press.

Heckman, J., & Masterov, D. (2004, April 14). "The Productivity Argument for Investing in Young Children." Working Paper

#5. Invest in Kids Working Group, Committee for Economic Development.

Herzenberg, S., Price, M., & Bradley, D. (2005). "Losing Ground in Early Childhood Education: Declining Workforce Qualification in an Expanding Industry, 1979-2004." Economic Policy Institute.

Gwen Morgan

Ms. Morgan has been at Wheelock College since 1972 as adjunct faculty, and as a leader in national research projects. Currently, she is Senior Fellow for Early Education and Care Policy. In her years in the field, Ms. Morgan has worked with others to found many new organizations, including: The KLH Child Development Center; The Advanced Management Seminars for Child Care Directors at Wheelock; The National Association of Regulatory Administrators (licensors); Work/Family Directions; Wheelock's Center for Career Development in Early Care and Education; The Child Care Action Campaign; and The Forum on Professional Workforce Development at NAEYC.

Suzanne Helburn

Ms. Helburn is professor emeritus of economics at the University of Colorado at Denver and was the coordinator and one of the principal investigators for the *Cost, Quality, and Child Outcomes in Child Care Centers Study*. She co-authored with Barbara Bergmann *America's Child Care Problem: The Way Out* (Palgrave for St. Martin's Press, 2002).

The Iron Triangle

A Simple Formula for Finance Policy in ECE Programs

by Louise Stoney

Early childhood program budgets, like all budgets, have two sides: the money coming in and the money going out. Balancing these two sides is essential, and is particularly challenging in the current recession economy. When seeking to balance their budgets, early childhood program directors typically focus on their rate — the price charged to parents or received as reimbursement from government. Rates are indeed important, however early care and education program income is also profoundly influenced by two other factors: enrollment and fee collection. These three factors form the 'iron triangle' of early care and education (ECE) finance. Paying close attention to the three sides of the iron triangle is key to sound fiscal management.

Full Enrollment

Almost all ECE revenue is tuition collected on behalf of an enrolled child. While government and philanthropy sometimes help finance ECE, this funding is rarely provided as general operating support; typically the dollars provided by third-party funders are linked to enrollment of specific children. If the children are not enrolled, the funding does not flow. This makes full enrollment a cornerstone of ECE finance, regardless of whether the program relies mainly on public funds or relies primarily on parent fees, or a combination. Unless a program is over-enrolled (a practice that is generally prohibited in licensing regulations because it could result in attendance that exceeds ratio and/or group size limits), it is not possible to operate at 100% enrollment. While some experts suggest that a well-run center can operate at 95% enrollment (Morgan & Emanuel, 2010), many suggest budgeting at a more achievable rate, such as 85% enrollment. Regardless of the target, any time enrollment drops below the budgeted target an ECE program is losing money.

Monitoring enrollment and acting quickly to address any shortfall is key to fiscal stability. This means program administrators must carefully track attendance, in each classroom, on a regular basis, and plan in advance when children will be 'aging out' of the program and/or moving to a different classroom. Without careful monitoring and active outreach to fill vacant slots, it is easy for these natural transitions to cause funding gaps. Tuition, especially when reimbursed by government, may also be dependent on actual attendance, so staying on top of this is crucial. It is easy for non-attendance to turn into non-enrollment. In a small program, every day a slot remains open can make a big difference. Over time these losses add up and can lead to serious financial shortfalls.

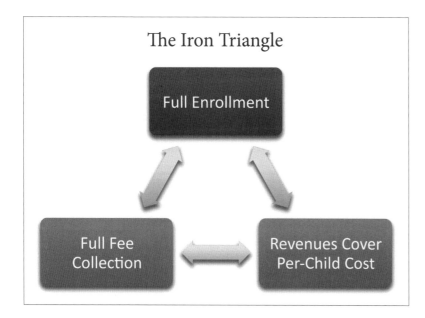

The Iron Triangle

Full Enrollment

Full Fee Collection

Revenues Cover Per-Child Cost

Full Fee Collection

Collecting fees — in full and on time — is essential. Fees only become revenue when they are collected. All too often an early childhood program will have a budget that balances on paper, but the cash just doesn't come in the door. Successful ECE administrators stay on top of fee collection; they have clear policies, are firm and consistent with families, thorough and prompt with billing, and on top of the paperwork required by third-party funders. Fee collection can be very time consuming unless systems are put in place to streamline and automate the process. Making electronic funds transfer (that is, enabling automatic transfer of funds from a bank account, debit or credit card) the norm for fee payment is one effective way to strengthen fee collection.

Revenues Cover Per-Child Cost

Setting tuition fees (prices) accurately involves many factors and decision points, some of which are beyond the control of an ECE program. What parents can afford to pay is based on what they earn and the local cost of living. What government, or other scholarship programs, will pay is typically based on available funds. That said, determining the

actual cost per child, comparing this cost to the price charged, and when fees cannot cover the full cost, identifying third-party funding to fill the gap, is essential to sound fiscal management. The bottom-line is that parent fees + third party payments must = per-child cost. Otherwise the program is losing money.

Both enrollment and fee collection impact actual per-child costs. If a program is not fully enrolled, the per-child cost increases. If bad debts go up (fees are not being collected), the per-child cost increases. In some cases, a budget gap can be addressed by boosting enrollment and/or lowering bad debt rather than raising fees. The three factors are interrelated. In tough fiscal times, when third-party funders are cutting budgets and parents are squeezed financially, ECE programs often face a difficult choice: keep fees high and risk increased vacancy rates and higher bad debt, or lower fees to boost cash flow. Unfortunately, the right answer is not simple or obvious, and it may vary from center to center based on the services offered and the families served.

The iron triangle is a simple formula for a complex issue. It can be a helpful way to stay on track, to remember what's important, but should not replace the many steps involved in sound fiscal management. Gwen Morgan and Bess Emmanuel have co-authored an excellent handbook, *The Bottom Line for Children's Programs: What You Need to Know to Manage the Money*, which should be an essential text for any program director involved in the business side of early care and education.

Reference

Morgan, G. G., & Emanuel, B. R. (2010). *The bottom line for children's programs: What you need to know to manage the money* (5th edition). Watertown, MA: Steam Press. Distributed by Gryphon House.

Louise Stoney

Louise Stoney is an independent consultant specializing in early care and education finance and policy and co-founder of both the Alliance for Early Childhood Finance and Opportunities Exchange. Louise has worked with state and local governments, foundations, national policy organizations, early care and education (ECE) providers, industry intermediaries, and child advocacy groups in more than 40 states and cities. In addition to leading the national Shared Services movement, Louise is currently using cost-modeling techniques to inform ECE finance, establish effective Quality Rating and Improvement System (QRIS) implementation, and craft innovative ECE policy. Louise writes occasionally for *Exchange* magazine, including: "The Iron Triangle: A Simple Formula for ECE Finance" (March/April 2013 issue), "First You Have to Pay the Bills: Training and Technical Assistance Focused on the Business Side of ECE" (September/October 2012 issue), and "Shared Services: A Powerful Strategy to Support Sustainability of ECE Businesses" (September 2009 issue.) Additional publications, among many, include: *Early Care & Education Compensation and Policy Options for Louisiana*; *Using Tax Credits to Help Finance ECE*; *Sound Business Management as a Key Ingredient of ECE*; and, *Shared Services: A New Business Model to Support Scale and Sustainability in Early Care and Education* (for the Kellogg Foundation); *Shared Services: Strengthening Early Care and Education* (for Communities & Banking, a publication of the Federal Reserve Bank of Boston); *Financing Child Care in The United States: An Expanded Catalog of Current Strategies* (for the Pew Charitable Trusts); *Smarter Reform: Moving Beyond Single Program Solutions to an Early Care and Education System*; and *Financing Early Childhood Care and Education Systems: A Standards-based Approach* (for Rice University). Copies of Louise's publications are available from www.earlychildhoodfinance.org or www.opportunities-exchange.org.

The True Cost of Quality in Early Care and Education Programs

by Billie Young

What's the gap between the price that families pay for child care and the 'true cost' of quality care?

Is there agreement among child care providers about elements of quality and what they cost?

If providers understood their budgets better and were clear about the funding they would need to reach the 'true cost' of quality, would they be empowered to advocate more successfully for increased funding?

Supposing parents understood the gap between the price they pay and the true cost — would they be willing to pay more? These questions were the catalyst for the True Cost of Quality project launched in the spring of 2001 by the City of Seattle's Northwest Finance Circle. The mission of the Northwest Finance Circle, a community collaboration, was to improve and expand the financing of early childhood and after-school programs by creating a new system of financing and by testing out innovative financing strategies. Over two years, we sponsored True Cost of Quality (TCOQ) budgeting classes for over 50 child care center directors and 16 family child care homes. The TCOQ project had two goals:

■ To get a better understanding of the gap between the current price of care and the cost of high-quality child care.

■ To help providers gain budget skills and become more powerful advocates for funding reform.

Believing the answers to our questions would be very different for family child care homes and child care centers, we developed TCOQ budgeting courses tailored to each group. This article will focus on our work with child care center directors.

Defining 'True Cost'

Job number 1 was defining 'true cost.' We brought together a group of skilled child care center directors to seek agreement on the elements and definition of 'true cost,' and to create a spreadsheet template.

The budget masters group was followed by three TCOQ classes, reaching over 50 child care center directors, who each prepared three budgets: current, true cost of quality, and ideal. TCOQ classes were seven weeks long, from 6:30 to 9 p.m., with dinner provided and stipends for directors who completed all three budgets. We analyzed their budgets to better understand the gaps between current costs, prices charged to families, and the true cost of quality.

Finally, we created and disseminated a toolkit that included a definition of TCOQ standards and Excel spreadsheets that directors could use to construct their own budgets.

Reaching Agreement on Standards

Our first hurdle was distinguishing between current, true cost, and ideal (or full cost) budgets. We had to help directors see the difference between the price they charge and the actual cost of care. Getting to true cost meant taking a giant leap — from their current costs to what it would take to provide high-quality child care every day.

A true cost budget was defined as the expense required to meet national accreditation standards (NAEYC and NASA[1]) on a consistent basis. Example costs included: classrooms consistently in ratio, reduced staff turnover, wages and benefits commensurate with those paid to others working in similar jobs, adequate facilities and equipment, funds for family support, professional development, office assistance, and release time for teachers to plan. True cost budgets included both ongoing costs to maintain the standards and one-time only costs needed to bring programs up to standard, such as facility modifications, playground construction, disability access modifications, and purchase of equipment such as computers.

In addition to accreditation, master budgeters agreed to the Model Work Standards created by the Center for the Child Care Workforce as the guideline for staff benefits and working conditions.

The debate over true cost intensified when it came time to set goals for wages. How much is 'too much'? We finally agreed to use the wage scale established for staff in state college child care centers, because they were developed as part of a Washington State Higher Education Commission comparable worth study in the late 1980s. True Cost course instructor Julie Bisson found that in every class, students vigorously debated about what people thought was 'reaching too high' for wages and benefits. They weren't sure it was feasible or even acceptable to use the state wage scale — even though it was mandated for state employees by the commission.

In the words of master budgeter Jennifer Hess, director of Blazing Trails, "It was a struggle to think beyond 'bare bones' and to get past our pride in doing so well with so little. We make something out of not enough every day. It felt like a true cost budget was asking for too much." We realized that we needed to ask directors to develop ideal budgets in order to put the true cost budget in perspective. Ideal budgets exemplified those expenses required to provide the best possible program — if there were no financial constraints.

Ideal budgets could include anything directors dreamed of, as long as it could be tied to standards of quality.

Examples of students' ideal costs included on-site nurses and therapists; outreach workers; coverage for teachers to do advocacy; an on-site sick room; art and music studios; grantwriters; and an emergency fund for families.

Bisson noted that students had trouble reaching for the possibilities — and even ideal budgets were modest in their dreams.

Directors Gained Valuable Lessons from True Cost Budgeting

Jodi Nishioka, TCOQ project coordinator, noted that students universally rated the class as valuable. "Many of the students had never prepared a budget, much less used Excel spreadsheets. Our most successful class was located in a computer lab, and we were able to help students learn how to use Excel during class."

Even though directors know that creating and monitoring budgets is a critical part of their jobs, it's hard to find the time to spend on a task that is perceived as hard and not a lot of fun. Diana Bender, one of the

TCOQ project coordinators, said, "It's like taking cod liver oil. You know it's good for you, but it's not a lot of fun to think about taking it — you kind of want to put off taking it as long as you can."

Fortunately, there were enough "ah-has" to keep directors moving through the process of creating not one, but three budgets. One director's big "ah-ha" moment was realizing that everything she cared about in early childhood was connected to financing; another's was realizing she was the lowest paid director in the room. She took the director salary survey students compiled in class to her board and got a raise! Other directors got peer support to build in modest annual increases in parent fees instead of fighting for big ones every few years.

On average, child care centers currently spend about 77% of their revenues on personnel, 1% on foregone revenue, 6% on occupancy, 6% on administration, and 10% on other costs. Reaching the true cost of quality would require increases of about 106%, with the biggest gap in wages. Average teacher wages in 2002 were about $9.94 an hour, while the true cost standard was $17.98.

Parents Can't Afford It, So We Can't Change It

True Cost instructors Julie Bisson and Juanita Bejaraños mediated the ever-present debate amongst directors: If we set our standards 'too high' will we price ourselves out of the market? What will happen to parents who can't afford the cost of true quality? We have to charge what it costs or we'll never be able to break the link and achieve quality for children. Bisson and Bejaraños brainstormed with directors on using their new budgets to motivate parents and boards of directors or owners to reach for quality-based budgets.

The debate about charging the true cost is overlaid with the realities of classism and racism. Programs in higher income neighborhoods could get closer to

---

Tips for Successful TCOQ Projects

- Design separate courses for centers and family child care.

- Try to pry students out of the minimalist 'box' in which child care providers dwell.

- Make time to debate definitions of true and ideal costs, and to reach agreement on shared standards.

- Afterschool requires two spreadsheets — for school year and summer — because revenue and staffing structures are unique.

- Access to a computer lab helps. Plan time to teach even experienced students to use spreadsheets. We found that about a third of the students didn't know how to read a budget and had never created one.

- Students may have math anxiety or 'budget phobia.' It takes a skilled instructor to demystify budgeting, help students talk about resistance and make it fun.

- Offer dinner, stipends for directors to complete all three budgets, and one-on-one mentoring for inexperienced directors.

- Spend time coaching directors to use budgets to advocate for change. Consider a buddy system for presentations to boards of directors and using a TCOQ invoice for parents that clearly identifies the gap between the price they are paying and the true cost of quality.

- Plan in plenty of time for directors for networking and learning from each other.

Jodi Nishioka and Diana Bender, TCOQ coordinators

the true cost of quality, while those serving low-wage families who were often families of color, felt stuck.

Jennifer Hess, director of Blazing Trails, said, "On the one hand, to reach quality we must pay good people well, and on the other, we have no program if we charge more than parents can pay. So we can't pay our staff worthy wages, and parents can't pay the already unaffordable fees."

Like many directors, Michael Brown of the NIA Center, faces tough realities. "I got a handle on our operating costs and what we'd really need to reach quality, but at the same time it was overwhelming. Programs with high numbers of children who are subsidized by the state are at the whim of government rates. You can't raise your rates enough to reach the True Cost levels and you hit a wall between your reality and your dream."

Jennifer and Michael are eloquent on the subject of true cost budgeting and the reality of closing the gap between price and the true cost of quality. We will never close the gap without systemic change in the way the United States finances child care. Creating that change demands persistent advocacy from parents and child care advocates, armed with the knowledge about the true cost of quality and united in a vision of quality for children and families.

Resources for True Cost Budgeting

- *Budgeting the True Cost of Quality Toolkit* by Julie Bisson. Available on the web at: www.ci.seattle.wa.us/ humanservices/fys/ TrueCostQualityCare/

- *Managing Money: A Center Director's Guidebook* by Roger Neugebauer and Bonnie Neugebauer, published by Exchange Press: www.childcareexchange.com

- *Model Work Standards, the Center for the Child Care Workforce*, www.ccw.org 16

Endnotes

1 NAEYC is the National Association for the Education of Young Children (www.naeyc.org); NASA is the National AfterSchool Association (www.nasa.org).

Billie Young

Billie Young, M.S.W., is manager of Child Development Programs for the City of Seattle and one of the founders of the Northwest Finance Circle. She is co-author with Jodi Nishioka of *Child Care is Not Child's Play: An Economic Analysis of the Child Care Industry in Washington State* (September 2004).

Four Good Reasons Why ECE is Not Just Important, but Essential

by Anne W. Mitchell

As new president, Barack Obama said in February 2009 in his first address to the nation:

" . . . [I]t will be the goal of this administration to ensure that every child has access to a complete and competitive education from the day they are born to the day they begin a career. Already, we have made an historic investment in education through the economic recovery plan. *We have dramatically expanded early childhood education and will continue to improve its quality, because we know that the most formative learning comes in those first years of life.*"

President Obama understands that we in the United States are part of the global economy and the global community. All of our children are important, in every nation on earth. He 'gets it' about the importance of the early years.

These words are music to the ears of any child advocate — "a complete education for every child from the day they are born" and "expand and improve the quality of early childhood education." Wow! It's been a long time since our national leaders were this articulate about early childhood education.

As early childhood educators and advocates, we know that early childhood matters. It's what we do every day with children; it's our life's work, and for many of us, it's our driving passion:

■ We know that learning happens through relationships.

■ We know that social and emotional development is directly linked with intellectual development.

■ We know that positive early learning experiences lead to later success in learning.

■ We know that families are the strongest influence on young children and when early childhood educators partner with families, children do better.

As advocates for young children and families and advocates for our profession — early childhood education — we have long argued for improving quality and for investing more public dollars:

■ We want higher standards for programs; that's why quality rating and improvement systems are sweeping the country and why thousands of programs in centers and homes are nationally accredited.

■ We want better and more accessible professional development, so that every teacher can advance their practice.

■ And most of all, we want overall greater public investment, per child, in early education so that we can achieve respectable compensation.

To make our case, we have used several different arguments alone or in combination.

The Moral Argument

We sometimes use the moral argument. Early education is a right for children. All children deserve great places to be every day and great people to be with. Children deserve good parents, good health, and good early learning experiences. Children deserve to have delightful and joyous childhoods that lead to bright futures. It's the right thing for society to invest in young children.

Families deserve support to raise children. After all, families are doing the work and paying to raise their children, who will grow up to become the leaders and workforce of tomorrow and support us all. The care of children that happens outside the early childhood education market, in families, is valuable to the economy. The feminist economist, Nancy Folbre, has written eloquently about these issues (Folbre, 1994, 2001, 2006).

As a society, we can help by investing in family supportive policies like paid family leave and family-supportive workplaces. Most nations (168 out of 173 in a recent report) have generous paid family leave for mothers (Heymann, Earle, & Hayes, 2007). Many provide paid leave for fathers as well as mothers. Only a few of our states have any paid family leave and the United States has no national policy.

The Workforce Productivity Argument

We are very familiar with the current workforce productivity argument and have used it for years. Parents need to work to support their families and they need dependable, quality programs for their children while they work. We usually add that employers benefit by having a dependable workforce, and that parents are more productive when they have good stable child care (Shellenback, 2004). Now we have good evidence that the benefits go well beyond the individual family and employer.

Investing in early care and education is an investment that strengthens the overall economy (Liu, Ribeiro, & Warner, 2004). In fact, higher quality is correlated with higher economic impact. Numerous economic impact studies have shown that early childhood education is a significant industry in every state, comparable to those that get a lot more economic development attention and public investment, such as tourism and hospitals.

A great resource with information on all 50 states is The Linking Economic Development and Child Care Project (see Resources).

Early childhood education is an industry that is worth about $50 billion nationally, and contributes to the economic health of local communities (Stoney, Mitchell & Warner, 2007). This money stays in the community; it is not a product that is shipped out and sold elsewhere. And early childhood education jobs are the jobs of the future — early childhood education is a service that people need that cannot be done electronically from any place in the world.

The Brain Research Argument

We've used the findings from neuroscience, or as we usually called it 'the brain research,' to make our case. The brain research argument is that the early years of a child's life, from the prenatal period onward, are when the brain is developing and growing faster than any other time. This period is critical and sets the stage for all of later learning and adult functioning. The baby's interactions with humans and the environment shape the brain's architecture. Positive and nurturing early relationships develop healthy well-functioning brains. As Jack Shonkoff and Deborah Phillips (2000) put it, "All children are born wired for feelings and ready to learn."

In those first months and years, the comfort, reassurance, and gentle stimulation that come through relationships with families and caregivers help babies and toddlers begin building self-control, persistence, curiosity, caring, and a sense of confidence. These are important concepts in their own right. They are precursors to essential skills that children will need to succeed in school and in life, such as emotional intelligence, empathy, ingenuity, conflict resolution, teamwork, and the ability to get along with others. A great resource on these issues is the Center on the Developing Child and their recent publication, *A Science-Based Framework for Early Childhood Policy* (see Resources).

The Return on Investment Argument

We have used the return on investment argument for a long time to argue that quality matters. The Perry Preschool and Abecedarian longitudinal research shows that high-quality early childhood programs have financial benefits much greater than their costs — investing in low-income young children is a good investment with high public returns. Recently, Nobel prize-winning economists such as James Heckman have delved deeply into this body of research, analyzed the accumulating evidence, and brought its conclusions to a larger audience than we can usually reach. Federal Reserve bankers like Ben Bernanke have become articulate messengers, propelling this argument onto the national stage.

We need to be careful in using this argument for two reasons: this evidence pertains primarily to low-income children, and it is high-quality that produces the positive long-term effects on children, not the quality of an average program. As advocates for all young children, we need to couple this argument with the facts about the benefits of early education for all young children (Barnet, Brown & Shore, 2004).

We also need to be clear about quality. There are three basic ingredients that make a high-quality program:

- **Structure:** small classes, enough adults, stable adults

- **Environment:** a supportive learning environment guided by well-designed curriculum

- **Process:** effective teachers who interact positively with each child, supported with professional development, reflective supervision, and good compensation.

This kind of quality costs.

The primary reason high-quality costs more is that better qualified teachers deserve to be paid well. College-educated workers command higher salaries and have options other than working in early education.

Lately, some in the early childhood research community have questioned the strength of the relationship between teacher credentials and program quality, and ultimately, child outcomes (Zaslow & Martinez-Beck, 2005). It is still absolutely true that higher levels of college education, that is, degrees, especially when the content is early childhood education, are generally related to higher program quality. The question is: exactly what level of education ensures high quality? A bachelor's degree? An associate's degree? The 'bachelor's degree debate' has been widely misinterpreted. It has been reduced to an either/or situation: either degrees matter or good training does.

Anyone who works in early childhood education, especially those who hire and supervise teaching staff, knows that the truth is *both* matter: the more educated you are, the better teacher you can be IF that education was specific to early childhood development and learning. And that reflective supervision, mentoring, and coaching — to implement what is learned in ongoing professional development — are what help teaching staff keep doing a good job.

A useful education focuses on how infants, toddlers, preschoolers, and primary grade children learn and grow, and how adults facilitate and promote children's learning and growth through interaction. A useful education is practical; it deals with real situations and has lots of fieldwork in real everyday settings where children are. Ivory towers don't produce good teachers. The real issue here is how we ensure that higher education is effective and practical and specific to early childhood. We need to make bachelors' degree programs better, not throw the bachelors out with the researchers' bathwater.

Finally, an important point that has been largely overlooked in this debate among researchers is that a college education has societal value that translates into economic value. Degrees are necessary if we are ever to achieve worthy compensation throughout this industry.

In an article entitled "Smarter Reform: Moving Beyond Single Program Solutions to an Early Care and Education System," my colleagues and I have combined all of these rationales into a coherent agenda (Stoney, Mitchell, & Warner, 2007). We call for financial support for institutions (the providers of early childhood education), financial aid for families, support for non-market care, and a publicly-funded infrastructure.

We have a President who has publicly committed to advance access to early childhood education and its quality. States are rapidly designing and implementing quality rating and improvement systems that provide a framework for unifying all the disparate sectors of early care and education. It's time to build the early learning system we need. Now is the time to use all four of these arguments to achieve greater public investment and good public policy for early learning. Let's start with the moral argument: It is right for society to invest in young children and their families.

References

Barnett, W. S., Brown, K., & Shore, R. (2004, April). The universal vs. targeted debate: Should the United States have Preschool for All? *NIEER Policy Brief* (Issue 6, April 2004) http://nieer.org/docs/index.php?DocID=101

Burchinal, M., Hyson, M., & Zaslow, M. (n.d.) Competencies and credentials for early childhood educators: What do we know and what do we need to know? *NHSA Dialog Briefs, 11*(1). Alexandria, VA: National Head Start Association.

Folbre, N. (2006). Rethinking the child care sector. Community Development. *The Journal of the Community Development Society, 37*(2): 38-52.

Folbre, N. (2001). *The invisible heart.* New York: The New Press.

Folbre, N. (1994). *Who pays for the kids?: Gender and the structures of constraint.* New York: Routledge.

Heckman, J. J., & Masterov, D. V. (2004). "The productivity argument for investing in young children" Working Paper. Invest in Kids Working Group, Committee for Economic Development, Washington, DC.

Heymann, J., Earle, A., & Hayes, J. (2007). The Work, Family, and Equity Index: How does the United States measure up? Project on Global Working Families: Boston, MA and Montreal, QC. www.nationalpartnership.org/site/DocServer/McGill_Study_2007.pdf?docID=1581

Liu, Z., Ribeiro, R., & Warner, M. (2004). *Comparing child care multipliers in the regional economy: Analysis from 50 states.* Ithaca NY: Cornell University Department of City and Regional Planning.

Shellenback, K. (2004). Child care and parent productivity: Making the business case. Ithaca, NY: Department of City and Regional Planning, Cornell University. http://government.cce.cornell.edu/doc/pdf/ChildCareParentProductivity.pdf

Shonkoff, J., & Phillips, D. (Eds.). (2000). *From neurons to neighborhoods: The science of early childhood development: A report of the National Research Council.* Washington, DC: National Academies Press.

Stoney, L., Mitchell, A., & Warner, M.E. (2006). Smarter reform: Moving beyond single program solutions to an early care and education system. *Community Development: Journal of the Community Development Society 37*(2): 101-15.

Zaslow, M., & Martinez-Beck, I. (Eds.). (2005). *Critical issues in early childhood professional development.* Baltimore: Paul H. Brookes Publishing.

Resources

The Center on the Developing Child
www.developingchild.harvard.edu
A Science-Based Framework for Early Childhood Policy

The Linking Economic Development and Child Care Project
http://government.cce.cornell.edu/doc/reports/childcare/

Anne W. Mitchell

Anne W. Mitchell is the President of Early Childhood Policy Research, an independent consulting firm specializing in evaluation, policy analysis, and planning on child care/early education issues with government, foundations, and national nonprofit organizations. She co-founded the Alliance for Early Childhood Finance. Previously she was Associate Dean of the Research Division at Bank Street College of Education in New York City where she directed the first national study of state-funded prekindergarten programs. She began her career directing child care centers in Massachusetts and Vermont. Anne has conducted national studies of state and local prekindergarten policy, Quality Rating and Improvement Systems, and early care and education finance; and has written widely on child care and early education policy and practice. She has an undergraduate degree in astronomy from Wellesley College and a master's degree in education leadership from Bank Street. Anne served 18 years as an elected member of the Greenville (NY) Board of Education, currently serves as treasurer of the Greenville Educational Foundation, and served five years on the New York State Professional Standards and Practices Board for Teaching. She has received leadership awards from the New York State Association for the Education of Young Children, the Bank Street College Alumni Association, Scholastic, Inc., National Louis University, the New York State Child Care Coordinating Council and the New York State and National Associations for Family Child Care. Anne is proud to be a Past President of the National Association for the Education of Young Children. She lives in Greene County near Albany, New York.

the Art of
LEADERSHIP

PROMOTING
EARLY CHILDHOOD SERVICES

2 CHAPTER 2
Advocating for Children and Families

Public Policy and You

by Eric Karolak

Have you ever met with an elected official to talk about the work you do? Have you ever written or called a legislator's office based on an action alert you received? Do you know the name of your Congressman and where he or she stands on child care? Do you wonder why people keep asking you these kinds of questions?

"Why does all this matter? It's all going on at the capitol and I have a program to run, children to care for…"

Elected officials make decisions that really do impact your day-to-day work as a child care provider. Many of the forms you fill out, trainings you attend, tuition assistance you receive, benchmarks you strive for, and processes you adhere to are because of a piece of legislation or regulation from Washington, DC, or your state capital.

Policies and You

As a child care teacher, you have the best insight, recommendations, and stories and experiences about what is really going on in your center or family child care home, and in your community. Your experience, training and education, and daily contact with children and parents make you a tremendous asset to the effort to get better policies for child care. The truth is you know more about children, child development, appropriate practice, and what makes a good program than many legislators. Legislators at all levels have competing priorities. It takes experts like you, and all of us working together, to keep them thinking about child care.

Got grants? Consider how a particular state or federal grant helps, for instance, and what the impact would be if you lost that grant, or heard the grant was expanding. Could you benefit? Would it matter? What would the rules for grantees be? Could you participate?

What if . . . ? If child care subsidy eligibility were cut in your state, how would that impact your program and the families of your community? What difference would a change in the market rate survey process or an increase in reimbursement rates make in your ability to provide your services?

Meeting higher expectations? Expectations for early childhood programs continue to increase in states across the country. Programs have to do more with less funding, and many initiatives require new and different standards. Consider what supports you and your colleagues need to meet those benchmarks.

What about Pre-K? Are you a child care provider participating in your state's prekindergarten program? What is that like? How does the state encourage and support Pre-K delivery in child care settings? Do policies address the needs of working families? What's the effect on infant and toddler care?

Are teachers supported? Do you have access to training, professional development, or educational opportunities? What are the requirements? How is it paid for?

These are all policies set by the federal or state government. Policies can and do change — often. Decision-makers need to hear from the people living with the real result of their decisions — you — about what is really going on. They need to hear the good, the bad, and the ugly. If something works, we certainly want to keep it. If something isn't playing out well, it's important to make a change.

You know that child care is complex; there are considerations to be made about the quality, the cost, the needs of children, parents, and child care providers, and the impact on the community. Our common goal is to provide the best possible care for children. Parents can't go to work without child care. Employers count on staff to show up, and entire economies depend on the business of business to carry on. Further, we know that a quality early learning and developmental experience makes a lasting impact on a child. Cognitive, social, and emotional development are critical to school readiness.

Why Now?

You've heard all this before. Now more than ever it's time to get involved in big ways or small ways, whatever you have time for. It all makes a difference. Early childhood education is getting more attention on the campaign trail than it has in years. Candidates at all levels know it is important to mention these issues. We need to help them follow through on their campaign ideas. Meanwhile, economic stress is impacting all of us and the programs we run. In tough fiscal times, it is still critical to share the story of how

important child care and early education programs are to children and communities. Priorities matter. Speaking up in tough times keeps legislators mindful that children should always be priority number one.

What Should We Do?

Legislators are people, too, and you may be surprised to find out how accessible they really are. They were elected to represent you and your community. Help them to truly do that by keeping them aware of what goes on in your neighborhood, city, and county.

There are many organizations that can be a source of information on policy advances at the state and federal level. You'll also find that child care teachers just like you are leaders in advocacy and can help you.

Advocacy doesn't have to be complicated or time consuming to be effective. There are many ways to get involved. The most important thing to remember is that you know best. It's time to let decision-makers know it.

Easy Ways to Get Started

■ Share your story: go to www.ececonsortium.org to tell us about the work you do.

■ Tell your friends to get involved.

■ Subscribe to a newsletter to find out about changing policies and ways to get involved.

■ Register to vote (and vote!).

■ Respond to an online action alert from an advocacy organization.

■ Write a letter to the editor — decision-makers read the hometown paper, too!

■ Go to work every day knowing that you are doing some of the most important work in the community, and that you make a difference.

Above all, stay informed. *Exchange* is committed to reporting on important national trends and developments in Washington, DC. In future columns, we'll look back on the 110th Congress, preview the future agenda for child care and early education, update you on critical issues for the early education workforce, quality initiatives, subsidy and prekindergarten, and connect those policies to real-world practice.

Eric Karolak

Eric Karolak is Chief Executive Officer of Action for Children, the source for child care and early learning services in central Ohio. Prior to returning to his native Ohio, Dr. Karolak was founding Executive Director of the Early Care and Education Consortium, a public policy alliance of thousands of early learning centers that together enrolled nearly 1 million children in all 50 states. From 2001 to 2006, he led the National Child Care Information Center, the largest federal clearinghouse focused on child care and early education. He has worked closely with states developing the technical aspects of child care assistance programs, quality rating systems, and partnerships across early childhood programs. He has conducted policy research and fiscal analysis in the areas of child welfare, child care, women's labor force participation, and public housing, and has testified before several state legislatures and both houses of the U.S. Congress.

Government Relations: It's Not Rocket Science

by Mike Radway

In the 1939 classic movie, *"Mr. Smith Goes to Washington"* Jimmy Stewart plays newly appointed Senator Jefferson Smith, an idealist who isn't afraid to stand up and speak out against a 'pork barrel' project to build a dam that will flood the proposed location for a national Boys Camp. After a lengthy filibuster and timely assistance from the *"Boy Rangers"* the forces of evil are vanquished and Senator Smith and his boys get their camp. Times may have changed since 1939, but the ability of good to triumph over evil in legislative battles has not, especially when the good guys have children on their side.

Many people in the early childhood education field are afraid of government relations work, intimidated by politicians, and believe the whole process is unseemly. They should not be afraid. Government relations is not rocket science. It relies on skills early care and education providers already have and use every day. They should not be intimidated because fundamentally officeholders are no different from the rest of us, and they, too, probably once needed our services. Finally, no right guaranteed by the first amendment to the U.S. Constitution should be regarded as unseemly; it is fundamental to our democracy.

How easy is government relations work? I started at the age of four (young enough to be a student in one of our centers) when my parents dressed me up as a politician for Halloween and sent me out to distribute flyers for our gubernatorial candidate. Even though my haul of Halloween candy may have been a little light that year, and even though my candidate lost, I've continued my government relations work for nearly half a century.

The skills you use to persuade an officeholder to support early childhood education are no different than the skills you already use to convince parents to send their children to your center. Be polite, friendly, and informative. Listen to their questions and respond to their concerns. Show off your center. Follow up. In their hearts, politicians want to support you just as parents want to send their child to your center — they just need you to reassure them they are making the right choice.

How do you find out who your local representative and senator are? Every state legislature and the U.S. Congress have tools on their websites that allows you to enter your address to find out who represents you. In most cases these websites provide direct links to the legislators' official websites, their email and regular mail addresses, and their phone numbers.

How do you get past the entourage of staff surrounding legislators so you can talk to them directly? There are several strategies for dealing with this issue. The first is to recognize that staff can be part of the solution, not just part of the problem. They are in their jobs because their bosses respect their opinions. Work with them and educate them as well.

The second strategy is to come armed with the three pieces of information a legislator is most likely to be interested in: How many children and/or families do you serve, how many employees do you have, and how much revenue do you generate for the local economy? Early childhood education is a major part of our economy; and if you are asking for a meeting with a legislator, remember that when it comes to government relations, your competitors are really your allies. They usually have the same concerns you have. It is okay to work with them, and multiple providers asking for a single meeting may have more success than single providers asking for multiple meetings.

The third strategy is to seek legislators out when they are in your area. If they won't come to you, you can seek them out. This isn't stalking, it simply means attending their town meetings, or going to public events like Rotary Club meetings, commencements, and ribbon cuttings.

I even ran into a Supreme Court Justice at the super-market once — although it is important to respect their privacy if they are with their family or at a personal and not a public event. Remember the "Golden Rule" ("Do onto others as you would have them do onto you"). Common sense tells you, for example, that it is never a good idea to lobby at a wedding or a wake.

What if you're still having trouble reaching your legislator? The old adage, "It's not what you know, it's who you know" needs updating. The reality is that what you know is important; it is a necessary, but not a sufficient, condition for effective government relations work. You also need to make sure someone hears what you are saying ("If a tree falls in the wilderness, does anyone hear it?"). That's where "who you know" becomes important.

It is not just enough, however, to think of whom you know. You also have to remember whom they know. The "Six Degrees of Separation" principle says that no two people on earth are more than six degrees of separation apart. That means that you should even be able to reach President Bush by going through no more than six intermediaries. The trick of effective government relations work is to get six degrees of separation reduced to one or two degrees so that someone you know (or someone they know) can make a meaningful introduction to an elected official for you.

Now you may doubt that you are less than six degrees of separation from President Bush, but the ease with which people can be connected to one another is convincingly demonstrated by a website called "The Oracle of Bacon" at the University of Virginia (www.oracleofbacon.org). The Oracle can tell you how many degrees of separation the actor Kevin Bacon is from 875,711 other actors and actresses. It will tell you, for example, that former President and actor Ronald Reagan is only two degrees of separation from Kevin Bacon because Ronald Reagan was in "The Young Doctors" with Eddie Alpert in 1961, and Eddie Alpert was in "The Big Picture" with Kevin Bacon in 1989. The average actor in the database is less than three degrees of separation from Kevin Bacon, and only 153 of the 875,711 (1/100th of 1%) are more than six degrees of separation from Kevin Bacon.

In short, you never know who you really know until you figure out who your friends and colleagues know, and who they know, and so on.

Once an introduction has been made and you have a chance to meet with a legislator or public official it is important to remember the KISS principle — "Keep it Short & Simple." Legislators and public officials lead very busy lives and have many demands on their time. Be respectful of their time constraints and try to get your point across as quickly and simply as possible. This is called an 'elevator speech' because it should take no longer than the 30 seconds it takes for a legislator to get from the first floor of the Capitol to the floor their office is on.

Imagine you are on an elevator and the Speaker of the House has just walked in. You have a very short time to introduce yourself and get your message across. Speak from your heart, and speak on behalf of the children and parents you serve. Try to include at least one memorable anecdote or fact. Be light-hearted if appropriate, but only if your humor does not seem forced. Tailor your presentation to your audience. Above all, remember that the route to success at the Capitol is the same as the way a musician gets to Carnegie Hall — practice, practice, practice!

Extend to legislators and public officials the same kind of courtesies you extend to parents and prospective parents at your center. Thank them for giving you their time. Listen to their concerns. If you don't know the answer to their question, offer to get back to them (and then do so). It is better to be frank and say you don't know than to guess the answer, be wrong, and prove you are either ignorant or untrustworthy. Remember to bring a handout you can leave behind so they do not have to take notes. Do not forget that the KISS principle applies to handouts as well — one page is better than two, two pages is better than three, and three or more pages is only better than none at all.

After your meeting send a thank you note, and, if available, artwork from a center in their district. It will make your visit more memorable and increase your chances of getting another meeting. Artwork I was given 32 years ago by students who wanted the Congressman I worked for to "Save the Whales" still hangs on my office wall today.

You do not have to have a pressing issue to visit with a legislator. It can be helpful just to introduce yourself, explain how your center helps families in their district, and let them know that you may be contacting them in the future when they are considering legislation that affects early care and education. They may be relieved that you are not asking for anything. If all you are asking for is a 'meet and greet,' let their

staff know that is all you need, and be respectful of the demands on their time and keep the meeting short.

Every time you meet with a legislator invite them to visit a center in their district. *No one can make a better case for you than the children at your center.* Every officeholder loves children, and loves having their picture taken with children. The children also usually enjoy the novelty of a visitor, especially an important one, and having a chance to show off what they know to someone new. Visits work best when there is genuine interaction between the officeholder and the children (e.g. reading, games, teaching, playing, even 'show and tell'). Visits create a perfect 'win-win-win' situation for you, for the children you serve, and for the officeholder. Politicians may forget office visits, but I guarantee you they never forget a visit to a center.

As Jimmy Stewart discovered in *"Mr. Smith Goes to Washington,"* children are our secret weapon. They are assets we have that very few other groups can match. The fact that their parents trust us every day with their most precious asset is a sign of faith and support that gives us unique credibility in the public policy arena. We must safeguard this asset as carefully as we safeguard the children who are entrusted into our care, but we should not be shy or ashamed to use that asset for the benefit of the children we love.

Resources

- Knowledge Learning Corporation, where lifetime learning begins®
www.knowledgelearning.com/

- Google, where you can find almost anything.
www.google.com

- Google News
www.googlenews.com

- Find your Representatives and Senators:
http://mygov.governmentguide.com/mygov/dbg/dbg/officials
http://stateline.org/live/News digests

Trade Association Resources

- Early Care and Education Consortium
  http://ececonsortium.org/

- National Child Care Association
  http://nccanet/org

- Alliance for Early Childhood Finance
  http://earlychildhoodfinance.org/

- National Association of Child Care Professionals
  http://naccp.org/

- National Association of Child Care Resource & Referral
  Agencies
  http://naccrra.org/

- National Association for the Education of Young Children
  http://naeyc.org/

- National Child Care Information Center
  http://nccic.org/

- Pre-K Now — an advocacy group
  http://preknow.com/

- National Association for Regulatory Administration
  http://naralicensing.org/

- National Institution for Early Education Research
  http://nieer.org/about/

Mike Radway

Mike Radway is the Senior Director of Government Relations
for the Knowledge Learning Corporation, which serves more
than 200,000 children in 39 states and the District of Columbia
through nearly 2,000 community centers, more than 500 school
partnership sites, and 123 employer-partnership centers. Prior
to working for KLC, Mike served as an appointee in both the
Clinton and Bush administrations, and worked for more than
two decades as a professional staff member on Capitol Hill. He
began his government relations work as a four-year-old trick-or-
treater in 1958 and has never looked back.

Mentoring Advocates in the Context of Early Childhood Education

by Sessy I. Nyman

Advocates have been a critical component in every social movement that effects change. Whether we examine the Civil Rights Movement, the Women's Movement, or the movement to create a public K-12 educational system, movements are made up of individual advocates. Types of advocates and how they create change vary greatly, but what ties them together is their common goal.

In the field of early childhood education, we have the foundation for an effective, broad-based coalition of advocates; there is much work to be done. Growing our advocacy community must be a high priority for everyone who cares for the future of young children — one advocate at a time. The work of each and every advocate is critical if we are to reach our goal of high-quality early learning and education for each child.

Advocates are People Who Bring an Issue to Life

There are no specific prerequisites for being an advocate. Most people advocate for something every day of their lives. It is in our nature when we believe in something or have a passion for the issue. The challenge lies in being an effective advocate — connecting the day-to-day work to a larger movement.

The Day Care Action Council of Illinois (DCACI) is a statewide advocacy organization, one of the few in the state to have a full-time lobbyist who works with elected officials to further an agenda that supports high-quality care and education for all young children. DCACI has a broad membership base of child care providers, parents, and other advocates. The strength of the agency does not lie only in its legislative relationships and policy know-how, but equally on it grassroots constituency.

In the spring of 2002, the Illinois Child Care Assistance Program faced drastic cuts that would have crippled child care providers and devastated low-income families already struggling to keep their children in high-quality programs. Over the course of 10 weeks, thousands of parents and child care providers across the state wrote letters, called their legislators, and rallied at the Capitol. In the end, no cuts were levied against the program — one of very few social service support programs that were not cut in a year of severe budget shortfall.

The key was not the access DCACI had to policy makers, nor was it the relationship DCACI had with community providers and parents statewide. Instead, it was the combination of both that made its advocacy efforts so effective. Individual advocate's actions were multiplied and made more effective because they were part of a larger campaign.

It is most effective when advocates come from a wide array of fields and interests to create a broad foundation for support. With a diverse foundation, an issue is brought to life for a variety of constituencies, in a variety of ways that more people can relate to and understand. Our challenge, as early childhood advocates, is to make the issue of high-quality care and education for young children everyone's issue. If it remains only our issue, we will never be successful.

In Illinois we have long worked to engage the business community as advocates for early care and education. Because they have a different constituency than either the typical parent or provider advocate, they speak from a business, workforce, or economic perspective of why child care matters. They often have networks and friends that early care and education advocates may not be able to access. Clearly, growing our advocacy community in numbers and diversity is critical to broad-based support and long-term change. Our goal is to make everyone an early childhood advocate: professional advocacy groups, researchers, elected officials, child care providers, pre-school and K-3 teachers, parents, community members, members of the business community, civic organizations, and unions. Many voices singing the same chorus is always more effective in creating change.

The Role of Mentors

Everyone has the capacity to be an advocate, but to be an effective advocate takes time and support. This is the role of the mentor in building advocates. Mentors can be many things to many people; the key is to be the right thing at the right time.

Any mentor, no matter what the issue or circumstance, needs to recognize the individual capacities of the person they mentor. One of the biggest mistakes a mentor can make is to measure one person against another, or worse, against himself. Just as there are

advocates from all walks of life, there are individuals with different levels of ability and commitment.

In its simplest form, the role of a mentor is to recognize each advocate's abilities and then build upon them. Understanding the starting point of a potential advocate will define the long process of mentoring the individual's potential.

Consider this scenario:

Sylvia was a life-long advocate now in a position to bring others along. She had been a central decision-maker to the children's movement, marched on Washington too many times to remember, established personal relationships with her local and national legislators, and effected change for children for over 20 years. She is a born advocate and wants to nurture future advocates and leaders for children. To her peers and fellow life-long advocates, Sylvia is a natural leader and thus, a natural mentor.

She is excited to share what she knows with others, so they, too, might become effective advocates for children. However, early on she became frustrated when a mentee did not participate in Saturday meetings, was unable to commit to national trainings, and did not feel comfortable speaking to large audiences. After a short time, Sylvia told her mentee that he did not have the qualities to be an effective advocate. She put the fault on the mentee, but the fault was in her skills as a mentor. A huge opportunity was lost.

From the beginning, Sylvia defined the criteria by her personal standards and skills; she did not begin with a clear understanding of the starting point for her mentee's emerging leadership. Instead of building a life-long advocate, she convinced a potential advocate that he didn't have what it takes.

To be an effective mentor, it is important to remember that the charge is not to clone yourself, but instead to identify skills and potential in the person you are mentoring and then to nurture the development of those skills. Sylvia could have nurtured the personal relationships the mentee already possessed, set up one-on-one meetings rather than creating large group settings, and built on the personal experience and knowledge of the mentee to help him begin to see his advocacy potential. In time, the confidence of the new advocate grows, and he or she looks for new challenges and opportunities for growth.

Ultimately, a mentor is charged with developing skills in a potential advocate, as well as:

■ helping 'beginner advocates' recognize that they are already advocates, and what they already do, however small, makes a difference.

■ helping grow and nurture advocacy efforts — looking not only at skill, but context and reach.

■ demonstrating to the advocate how his or her efforts fit into a larger movement.

■ helping the advocate identify key relationships they currently have, and encouraging them to establish new relationships that will extend the reach and impact of their work.

■ supporting the advocate in the pieces of advocacy that are new, until the advocate feels comfortable doing it on his or her own.

■ encouraging every advocate to be a leader and continually reaching out to engage new advocates committed to the same goals.

Part of a Movement

In reality we are all part of a state, national, and even international movement that supports high-quality care and education for all children. This is a big concept for many advocates to get their arms around. It is always important to be aware of the larger movement or vision, while at the same time making the issue local and real. When an issue has immediate impact on local children, it is much easier to build a broad base of support.

All advocates must be part of a movement, group, or network that can directly affect public policy. Policy is the primary way to create overarching, long-lasting change. While the work that happens in our neighborhood, our school district, or our town are all important, unless they connect to the larger public policy process, real change will not occur.

What an Advocate Needs

Passion is the essence, the necessary requirement for advocacy. It provides the essential foundation upon which other advocacy skills can be built. A review of the following list can help gauge an advocate's skill and knowledge level, whether the advocate is you or someone you are mentoring. Knowing where you are at the beginning points you in the direction of where you need to grow — this is an important first step in mentoring an advocate.

■ **Understanding the issue.** Many advocates understand the issue from their own perspective or experiences. However, in order to build support and ownership of the issue among others, understanding the entire issue, with all its complexities, is critical. It is essential to be able to explain the issue and its importance to people who might not be early childhood professionals or who do not have young children.

■ **The context.** Knowing at least part of the history of an issue is critical to mapping out where it will go. Why has ECE emerged today as such an important issue? What has changed to increase demand? How have our expectations changed for young children? What is the role of ECE?

■ **Messaging.** The work of creating a message or building support happens in two primary categories:

• Creating public will is central to the work of an advocate. If the general public does not support a concept or an issue, then the chances that change will happen are slim. Having a broad range of support and demonstrating need and effect is important in building public will.

- Creating political commitment largely depends on the ability to create public will and to make sure elected officials know that the public supports the issue. We do this in a variety of ways, including relationship building, networking, public education, and media exposure. Just as it is important that advocates individually work towards a common goal, so, too, is it critical that the work comes together in a common message.

- ■ **Relationship building.** Relationships are built over time by establishing trust, respect, and common interests. Whether engaging an elected official, other advocates, parents, or community members, relationships are crucial to an advocate's success. Understanding that a relationship goes beyond the current issue or campaign is critical for a new advocate.

Ten Commandments of Policy Advocacy

- Start with a base. Your base should reflect the breadth and diversity of support for your issue.

- Work on a bi-partisan basis. This is the only way to avoid gridlock between the two chambers and the executive.

- Cultivate a legislative champion in each house. Advocates, grassroots supporters, and lobbyists can only do so much; the sponsor must be a committed advocate when the legislation is debated.

- Create a simple message that explains your issue, and then make sure that your supporters repeat it, over and over again.

- Develop human-interest stories to demonstrate your points. Do not underestimate the power of anecdotes.

- Organize a creative coalition in support of the issue. The most effective coalition partners lend an element of surprise; they are not expected to support the issue and may have opposed you before.

- Activate your grassroots support. Legislators care most about issues that affect their own constituents. At the state or local level (not Congress), their unique letters or telephone calls create an impression of widespread support or opposition on all but the most controversial issues — on the same theory that ten cockroaches in a kitchen appear to be an infestation.

- Be ready to compromise. No policy of government ever looks the same as when it was proposed.

- Never lie or mislead a policy maker about the importance of an issue, the opposition's position or strength, or any other matter. Your word is your bond.

- Use the media to focus on public debate and to generate interest in the issue. Legislators and policy makers are especially sensitive to media approval and criticism.

Prepared by Julie E. Hamos and Associates, September 1998

■ **Understanding the players.** Who are the players? They are anyone and everyone you interact with, who cares about your issue, who is effected by your advocacy work, or even who might take a contrary view of your issue. They are also the leaders on your issue — the people making decisions, the people who people listen to, and the people who have made a difference in the past. While everyone is important in turning an issue into policy, the players are the faces that the general public connects with the issue.

■ **Why should anyone else care?** Early childhood care and education affects every segment of our society. An effective advocate will be able to explain how the issue affects different populations in different ways. The reasons why a parent cares about early childhood care may be different from why the local Chamber of Commerce cares. Both are important. The cost-benefit model of investing in quality early care and education is just as compelling to some legislators as the new research on brain development in infants is to others. By working with advocates from various fields, you learn how to craft your message in order to reach a variety of populations which helps you to ultimately be successful.

Thinking of advocacy skills in these ways will enable a mentor to help advocates recognize their skills and potential, and then to nurture strengths, overcome weaknesses, and understand the context.

Mentoring Change

Change happens in a variety of ways, and a good mentor can ensure that each venue and opportunity for advocacy is the most effective it can be. As a young person entering the world of community activism and advocacy, I needed the leadership, guidance, and inspiration of mentors so that I could see my potential and the possibilities for change.

It is appropriate to write this article now, as the climate in our nation is not one conducive to highlighting the deficiencies in our various systems.

States are facing major budget shortfalls, and critical services like child care and other early learning opportunities are being cut; some to the point of their collapse.

This is also a time of great opportunity for change. There is a national awakening around the importance of early brain development and the critical impact of high-quality early learning opportunities for children from birth to five. There is growing concern in the business and education communities that if we don't invest in our very youngest learners, then we can never expect to have successful students and productive professionals in the future.

Now is the time to become an advocate, mentor an advocate, and grow our community of advocates for high-quality early learning for all children.

Sessy I. Nyman

As the Vice President of Policy and Strategic Partnerships, Sessy Nyman directs state and federal legislative strategy and coalition building for Illinois Action for Children. Her leadership and advocacy efforts have contributed to an increase of state resources invested in early care and education by more than $160 million. In addition to negotiating legislative outcomes and spearheading administrative advocacy to state agencies, Nyman manages statewide campaigns for policy change and increases in fiscal expenditures; creates partnerships with community organizations, parents, and faith-based initiatives; and develops grassroots organizing activities and strategies. She has a long-standing professional history in advocating for vulnerable populations, including her work as the Director of the Violence Prevention Project for the Alliance for Logan Square Organizations. Nyman earned her master's degree in Cultural Geography from The University of Massachusetts – Amherst and holds a bachelor's degree in Government and International Relations from The University of South Carolina. She resides in Chicago with her husband and daughter.

Cutting Through the Red Tape

Strategies for Dealing with Bureaucrats

by Roger Neugebauer

"Bureaucracy is a giant mechanism operated by pygmies."
Honore de Balzac

The term *bureaucrat* conjures up the stereotype of a nit-picking, regulation spouting, heartless, bumbling paper-pusher. Yet bureaucrats no more fit a single mold than do child care directors or teachers. Some are rigid, others are flexible; some are brilliant, others are insipid; some are dedicated, others are self-serving.

What gives rise to the stereotype is that certain characteristics of life in the bureaucracy force employees to conform to standard and structured routines in performing their jobs. This article will describe these characteristics and how they affect bureaucrats' relationships with outside agencies. It will then outline some strategies for dealing with the types of bureaucrats child care directors are likely to encounter.

Life in the Bureaucracy

Bureaucracies provide little motivation to work hard. Individuals typically come to work for bureaucracies sincerely committed to making an impact in their field. However, new employees' expectations of becoming involved in shaping major policies and in planning exciting new programs are soon dashed. New policies and programs are generally developed at the highest levels of the bureaucracy and then turned over to the lower levels to enforce or administer. One welfare official lamented:

"I hoped to use my expertise to help improve services for children. But instead I spend all my time tracking down lost payments, reviewing budget revisions, clearing audit reports, and running around getting 18 sign-offs on contracts. My master's degree in child development is irrelevant; I should have gotten one in paperwork."

Bureaucracies also provide little recognition for quality performance. Bureaucrats typically are responsible for monitoring or processing a workload of projects, contracts, or programs. If they fall behind in their production, they may receive considerable negative recognition in the form of pressure to produce from their superiors. However, if they manage their work on a timely basis, their work tends to be taken for granted.

What the bureaucracy focuses on is quantity, not quality. What is important is how many licenses are renewed or how many contracts are approved, not the quality of care children are receiving in those programs.

Given the emphasis on paperwork and processing, bureaucrats are seldom required by the bureaucracy to exercise their professional skills. If they take an interest in improving quality of services, it is because their own personal standards demand it or because they are receiving recognition or support from outside the bureaucracy for doing so.

A contract representative may work particularly hard to gain full funding for high-quality programs, a welfare official may advocate the adoption of a sliding fee scale, or a licensing official might provide technical assistance to centers struggling to survive. Such efforts generally go unrewarded by the bureaucracy.

Bureaucracies pressure bureaucrats to conform. Bureaucracies manage routine work best — work to which the established rules, process, and schedules can be applied. When something comes along that causes the bureaucracy to move outside its routine procedures, this causes problems and is resisted.

Thus, a bureaucrat advocating a procedural waiver for an innovative program or for the revocation of a particularly bad center's license will likely encounter resistance and resentment. Bureaucrats who regularly push for changes, exceptions, and quality services are soon labeled as troublemakers.

The pressures on a troublemaker to conform are considerable. The most effective pressure is that the more a bureaucrat inconveniences his co-workers by seeking non-routine actions, the harder it becomes to overcome their resistance and gain their support. A more long-term pressure is the fact that superiors will not actively fight for promotions for troublemakers. Those who conform with the routines are rewarded with promotions.

In addition, reassignment of duties is a common ploy for discouraging troublemakers. A social services worker who gets actively involved in advocating rate increases for centers may be reassigned

to process Medicaid claims or to work in an undesirable geographic location. Finally, superiors can grind troublemakers into submission by rigidly enforcing office procedures — for example, personal phone calls may be forbidden and pay may be deducted for taking five minutes too long on a break.

"Bureaucracy defends the status quo long past the time when the quo has lost its status."
Laurence J. Peter

Not surprisingly, the vast majority of bureaucrats eventually succumb to this pressure to conform. Many spirited advocates (see box) have been cowed into becoming pseudo-advocates who chant the clichés of their causes, but who no longer have the heart to fight the bureaucracy for them.

Bureaucracies reward outside agencies that conform to their routines and standards. The treatment outside agencies receive from a bureaucracy is largely determined by the extent to which they conform to the bureaucracy's established procedures. The likelihood of an agency's request being approved often has more to do with the way the agency fills out the forms than with the quality of services it provides. Requests, which cannot be handled routinely, cause inconvenience to bureaucrats. The tendency for the bureaucracy is to delay acting on such requests, to reject them on a technicality, or to return them for clarification.

The treatment an agency receives may also depend upon the extent to which it conforms to unofficial standards for good programs. Bureaucracies generally have neither the inclination nor the resources to fully evaluate providers' services. As a result, quality judgments are often based upon stereotypes and labels. Oftentimes a program will be reacted to as good or bad depending upon whether it is for-profit or non-profit, small or large, part-day or full-day.

In other situations, a bureaucrat may label an agency depending upon his personal relationship with the director, the extent to which the agency complies with his requests, or the physical appearance of the agency's

Four Types of Bureaucrats

Climbers

- Seek to maximize their own power, income, and prestige through increased rank and authority
- Tend to enforce or ignore agency rules depending upon what best suits their personal interests
- Promote reorganizations and changes, which provide them with opportunities to increase their power base
- Insert themselves in the center of decision making wherever possible

Advocates

- Seek to promote specific causes by fighting on their behalf from within the bureaucracy
- Work to promote decisions favorable to their cause by coordinating pressures from inside and outside the bureaucracy, as well as by winning over key decision makers
- Bend, stretch, and ignore agency rules on behalf of their cause and look for loopholes or seek revisions in rules that are disadvantageous
- Constantly fight for changes in agency policies and structures that further their causes

Conservers

- Seek to maximize their security and convenience through maintaining their current position and income
- Escape responsibility for decision making so as not to risk making bad or controversial decisions
- Rigidly apply agency's rules, exercise minimal personal discretion, and try not to rock the boat
- Oppose organizational changes that might threaten their position

Pseudo-advocates

- Sympathize with specific causes, yet are unwilling or unable to promote them in the bureaucracy
- Complain about decisions that hurt their cause, but do not work hard to influence them
- Enforce agency rules while claiming they disagree, but are powerless to change them
- Constantly talk about the need for changes, but do little to actively promote them

This classification is derived from one proposed by Anthony Downs (see Credits), but modified on the basis of the author's experience.

facility. Such labels, once established, are communicated to co-workers and are slow to change.

Bureaucracies unofficially delegate operational decisions to the lowest levels. While bureaucrats at the lowest levels are virtually powerless to influence the bureaucracy's policy development, many do exercise considerable control over the day-to-day decisions. First-line bureaucrats, those who deal directly with the outside agencies, in large part determine the outcome of requests from these agencies. They seldom have the authority to make any final decisions, but their recommendations on routine, non-controversial decisions are generally adhered to by their supervisors.

Supervisors commonly handle four to ten workers, each of whom may work with ten or more outside agencies. Therefore, the supervisor cannot possibly be familiar with all the requests from all the agencies and must, of necessity, rely on the opinions of the workers.

First line bureaucrats' strongest power is of a negative kind. While they may have a difficult time gaining approval for requests, they can easily prevent their approval. They can make a recommendation that a request be denied, which will be difficult to reverse unless the requesting agency has supporters in the higher echelons. They can delay processing a request until a deadline has passed. They can pester the agency interminably for additional information or revisions. If all else fails, they can lose the paperwork.

"I do not rule Russia; ten thousand clerks do."
Nicholas I

Strategies for Dealing with Bureaucrats

Be a friend — not an antagonist. For many bureaucrats, the most, if not only, satisfying aspect of their work is their relationships with the organizations and individuals they deal with outside the bureaucracy. If a bureaucrat derives satisfaction from a pleasant professional relationship with a child care center, she will be motivated to work hard to see to it that the center's requests receive fair and expeditious treatment. If she is irritated or offended by the center, she will be more likely to exercise her negative powers.

■ **Establish rapport with bureaucrats.** Don't treat them like impersonal cogs in a giant machine. Show concern for their personal interests.

■ **Give them a tour of your program.** Invite them to lunch with the children. Introduce them to your staff, board members, and parents.

■ **Keep in touch regularly, not just when you have a problem or need money.** Invite them to special occasions (Thanksgiving dinners, annual meetings, carnivals). Send them regular progress reports, newsletters, and announcements.

■ **Show your appreciation for their work on your behalf.** Thank them personally. Write a letter to their supervisor to let them know what a good job they are doing.

■ **Strive for fairness, not favoritism.** If it becomes apparent that you are befriending a bureaucrat in hopes he will ignore a blatant licensing violation or push through an unnecessary budget increase, this will more likely rub his ego the wrong way and cause him to work against you. An attempt to buy a bureaucrat's unquestioning support through wining and dining is also more likely to backfire than not.

Make bureaucrats your advocates. Since bureaucrats receive little professional stimulation from pushing papers inside the bureaucracy, they often welcome opportunities to become involved in providing technical assistance to service providers. (It's an irony of the field that frustrated bureaucrats long to work in centers where they can be directly involved providing services, while burned-out directors seek to move into bureaucracies so they can have a broader impact on programs and policies.) It is especially helpful to get their assistance in shaping projects or proposals, which will be submitted to the bureaucracy. Once they have an ego involvement in a request, they are not likely to let it die easily.

■ **Don't show bureaucrats only your center's bright spots.** Share your problems with them and get their advice on solutions. Ask them how other centers they work with are handling these problems.

It can be particularly helpful to gain the bureaucrat's support when the problem is the result of her bureaucracy's policies or procedures. She may be able to find loopholes, waiver procedures, or other proper means of getting around the problem. If not, having seen the effect of a policy on a center, she may be motivated to advocate from within for changing the policy.

■ **When preparing requests to the bureaucracy (applications for a license renewal, funding proposals, annual financial reports), seek the advice of the bureaucrats.** Twenty minutes spent going over a proposal with a bureaucrat before it is filed may save weeks of delays caused by filling it out improperly or by not explaining certain sections fully enough.

If your center is about to file an unusual request (such as a major mid-year budget revision or a waiver request for a particular licensing requirement), the bureaucrat may be able to suggest ways of framing the request that are least likely to cause conflict with the bureaucracy's standard routines and procedures.

■ **Give bureaucrats opportunities to become involved in major policy debates.** Invite them to participate in local coalitions or associations, which are active in advocacy around policy issues. If they can be fired up about the importance of certain policy changes, they are more likely to act as advocates for policy reform within the bureaucracy. Advocates within the bureaucracy who are not inspired and supported from the outside soon lose their enthusiasm and become pseudo-advocates.

Don't become too dependent upon individual bureaucrats. While it is vital to gain the understanding and support of the bureaucrats who deal directly with your center, it can be a mistake to rely solely on their support. No bureaucrat is going to care about your center as much as you do. While they may support your requests, given the many pressures they are under, they may not push your requests as aggressively as you might wish.

■ **Become thoroughly informed about how the bureaucracy functions.** Find out the names and responsibilities of all the individuals who handle your request. Become thoroughly familiar with the rules and procedures that affect your center. Don't

rely on bureaucrats to interpret the rules for you. Find out which rules can be waived and who has the authority to waive them. Talk to other directors and find out the various ways in which unclear rules have been applied.

■ **Get to know all the decision makers personally in the bureaucracy.** Make a point of introducing yourself to the head of the organization, as well as to the secretaries, auditors, financial analysts, and other technicians who may handle your center's requests. If they know you personally, it is somewhat less likely they will treat a request from you as just another piece of paper to push. Also, they will be more likely to listen and give you an honest answer when you call in to check on the status of a request.

■ **Develop a contact in the bureaucracy who will give you an accurate report on the status of your requests.** It is best, of course, if you can develop sufficient rapport with the first-line bureaucrats who deal with you directly so that they will always give you honest reports. If you are dealing with a climber, a conserver, or a pseudo-advocate, however, you may find that they cannot be relied upon. They may say, for example, that a budget revision is being held up in another office while in fact it has been sitting on their desk for a week. If this is the case, it behooves you to make a friend in the bureaucracy who can provide reliable reports. Don't be reluctant to develop such contacts. You are not seeking inside information — you are seeking information that you are fully entitled to have.

Know how and when to apply pressure. Oftentimes developing a good working relationship with a first-line bureaucrat will not be enough to ensure that your center is treated fairly by the bureaucracy. Your license renewal may be rejected over a questionable interpretation of a rule, your school lunch reimbursement claim may be delayed unreasonably long, or you may be required to submit unnecessarily detailed financial reports. In such instances, it may be necessary to apply some pressure on the bureaucracy. However, if pressure is applied at the wrong time or in the wrong place, this could do more harm than good.

Guidelines for Bureaucrats:
(1) When in charge, ponder.
(2) When in trouble, delegate.
(3) When in doubt, mumble.
— James H. Boren

■ **Don't make a cause célèbre out of every minor delay and setback.** An organization that develops the label of chronic complainer will soon find the bureaucracy turning a deaf ear on its complaints. Regular phone calls to politely inquire on the status of your requests are more likely to prevent routine delays.

■ **Avoid alienating bureaucrats.** Similarly, if you have developed a good relationship with and are receiving generally good service from a first-line bureaucrat, it is not in your best interest in the long run to alienate this bureaucrat by going over his head when an isolated breakdown does occur. A more effective strategy would be to consult the bureaucrat directly. Ask him where the delay or problem is and get his advice on how you can most effectively bring pressure to bear. If, on the other hand, you find that you are receiving consistently poor service from the first-line bureaucrat assigned to your center, you should request that a different individual be assigned. Ask for a meeting with the field representative's immediate supervisor. Cite specifically how in case after case the bureaucrat in question has failed to act responsibly on your requests, supplied you with inaccurate information, or failed to inform you of deadlines and policy changes.

■ **When it is time to apply pressure, it is best to attack with facts, not emotions.** A display of righteous indignation may be effective in gaining the attention of the head of the bureaucracy; but in the final analysis, it will be the facts you present that will influence her decision. If you are complaining about unnecessary delays and red tape, you should document the date your request was

---

Understanding Bureaucratize

Conservers and pseudo-advocates tend to convey unpleasant news with obtuse stock phrases so as to avoid the inconvenience of having to assuage angry clients. The following examples demonstrate how to interpret such phrases.

This looks good to me, but I'll have to clear it through the front office.

Translation: Your proposal stinks, and I plan to reject it, but I'd prefer you to think it was my boss who shot it down.

You mean you haven't received our answer yet?

Translation: I haven't done a thing on your request, but I'd prefer you to think I had and that the post office lost our reply.

I don't make the rules — I just carry them out.

Translation: I could have fought to get a waiver to approve your request, but it was so much easier for me to simply reject it.

He'll be in conference all day or
He's away from his desk now.

Translation: He hasn't even looked at your budget revision yet, but he doesn't have the guts to tell you that.

---

submitted, as well as the dates you contacted the bureaucracy by letter or phone seeking a status report, who responded to your inquiry, and what they said. If you are protesting an unfair decision, go to the rules and regulations and demonstrate why the decision was not appropriate. Also cite examples of how in the past or in other jurisdictions the opposite decision was made on similar cases.

■ **Give the bureaucracy a means of saving face.**
Bureaucrats, like everyone else, have egos and prefer not to admit publicly that they made a mistake. Superiors don't like to alienate their staffs by publicly criticizing their actions or inactions.

Don't demand that a decision be reversed; rather ask that it be reconsidered on the basis of new information that you are supplying (even if you are only restating or clarifying what was presented initially). Even be prepared to offer to make some minor changes in your position so that the bureaucracy can announce that a compromise was reached. Give them a means of making a graceful retreat.

"We can lick gravity, but sometimes the paperwork is overwhelming."
Wernher von Braun

Credits

Altshuler, A. (1977). *The politics of the federal bureaucracy.* New York: Harper and Row, Publishers.

Boren, J. H. (1972). *When in doubt, mumble: A bureaucrat's handbook.* New York: Van Nostrand Reinhold Company.

Downs, A. (1973). "Inside bureaucracy: Five types of bureaucrats." In H. J. Leavitt and L. R. Pondy (editors), *Readings in managerial psychology.* Chicago, IL: University of Chicago Press.

Roger Neugebauer

Roger Neugebauer is founding publisher of *Exchange Magazine* and a co-founder of the World Forum Foundation.

How to Take a Meeting with Policy Makers

by Jeffrey Capizzano and Molly Fishman

As a former Senior Policy Advisor for Early Childhood Development and Education at the US Department of Health and Human Services (HHS) and a current Legislative Aide for Senator Michael Bennet of Colorado, we have taken a lot of meetings with early childhood stakeholders. In many cases, we left these meetings feeling energized and empowered, either having learned something that informed our work, brainstormed an innovative idea, or came up with a solution to a problem. In other cases, we left not understanding why the meeting needed to take place, the stakeholder's perspective, or how to be helpful going forward.

Those who represent you in Washington, DC place a high value on the opinions and experiences of stakeholders. They want to know how current and proposed legislation and regulations affect the work that you do and are always seeking recommendations from constituents regarding how things can improve. Typically, if you are meeting with a policy maker in Washington, it is because:

■ you are looking to spread the word about your work.

■ a policy is negatively impacting your ability to be successful.

■ you have an idea for a policy change, or an opinion on a current policy proposal.

Regardless of the reason or whether they are on Capitol Hill or with the Administration, we want your meetings to be successful. And while there is no one right way to take these meetings, there are certain norms and expectations that, if understood, will make them more effective.

Below, we highlight some of the common issues that make meetings less effective and offer strategies to make the most of the time you have with actors in the policy world.

Common Issues that Make Meetings in Washington Less Effective

In thinking about meetings that went particularly well, and those that did not, a common set of issues come to mind.

No "Ask"

An "Ask" is an inside-the-beltway expression for the reason why the meeting is taking place. Put simply, it is what you need to happen as a result of the meeting. For example, an "Ask" could be:

- "I have a great idea and I need help identifying sources of funding."

- "I'm having a problem with an agency and no one is returning my calls. Could you help?"

Although it seems obvious that one would have an "Ask," it is surprising how many meetings end without one.

An "Ask" outside of the staff's purview

Policymaking is complex, and given how much occurs every day in Washington, work is divided among staff. Typically, a staffer will be assigned a set of issue areas (e.g. health and education) or to a specific initiative (e.g. Race to the Top — Early Learning Challenge grant program). At higher levels, an official might have authority over your issue area (among many), but lack detailed knowledge in the area. In this case, you hope that the senior official pulls in the appropriate staffer to provide support, but this does not always happen. Unfortunately, given this level of organizational complexity and division of labor, stakeholders can often find themselves making an "Ask" of someone with no jurisdiction over that particular area.

Correct "Ask," but unprepared for follow-up questions

Even when there is a clear "Ask" of the right person, stakeholders can be unprepared for follow-up questions such as:

- "Can you tell me about the evidence that shows that this works?"

- "How much would it cost if we . . . ?"

- "How does this align with the Senator's priorities for early childhood education?"

Follow-up questions are generally a good sign, indicating how well the policy actor understood the issue and their level of engagement, but you must be prepared. Typically, these are not difficult questions to anticipate and require just a basic understanding of what the person you are meeting with is working on and the questions he or she might get asked when presenting 'up the chain.'

Strategies to Make Meetings in Washington More Effective

Finding the right person

Most of the important work for a Washington meeting happens before you set foot in an office. In the pre-meeting phase, you develop your message or inquiry (the "Ask") and do your research to ensure that the message finds the right person. If you are unsure where to start, visit www.senate.gov and www.house.gov to find your Senator or Representative. The websites of specific Senate and House offices are typically: lastname.senate.gov and lastname.house.gov. At the bottom of a Member's homepage, you will find the contact information for the Washington, DC offices.

When you call to set up a meeting, let the office know:

- you will be traveling to DC during a certain time period and would like to schedule a meeting.

- you would like the email address for the scheduler who will set up the meeting.

- you would like the name of the staffer who handles early childhood issues.

- you would like the spelling of both staffers' names.

Although front offices are usually not allowed to give out staff email addresses, Senate and House email addresses follow a specific convention, so it is fairly easy to email policy makers and their staff once you have their names. Senate email addresses follow the format of *firstname_lastname@senatorslastname.senate.gov* and House email addresses are typically *firstname.lastname@mail.house.gov*.

Your first email after your call to the office is to the scheduler. Keep this email short (no longer than a paragraph) and include:

- your name, title, and affiliation/organization.

- purpose of your email.

- the person with whom you would like to meet (e.g. the Senator/Representative if available or the staffer who handles early childhood issues).

- your preferred meeting date/time (while communicating that you are flexible).

- the best way to reach you (preferably an email address).

For the most part, meetings with Administrative agencies are handled in much the same way, although it is sometimes harder to find the right person to talk to. The Department of Education's (ED) Office of Early Learning and HHS's Office of Early Childhood Development are good staring places.

As with any meeting, the farther in advance you begin the process, the better. It is important to remember that offices receive numerous meeting requests, so do not worry if you do not hear back immediately. Follow up on the initial request with a second email about five days later (if your trip is sooner, wait two to three days before sending another email).

Developing Your "Ask"

When developing your "Ask," first focus on your policy goal and how the meeting helps you achieve it. Are you meeting to introduce yourself and your organization? Do you want to express your support or disapproval for a piece of legislation? Second, figure out how to make it relevant to the person with whom you are meeting. Ideally, your "Ask" should be tied to the current legislative agenda and framed in terms of the policy maker's goals. As early childhood professionals, we teach children about empathy — understanding another person's point of view and feelings. This is a somewhat analogous process, finding the interests of the person with whom you are meeting and talking about your work from their perspective.

To gain insight into what may be influencing or 'on the radar' of the person with whom you are meeting, you should research entities that have jurisdiction over early childhood issues, including the Senate Committee on Health, Education, Labor, and Pensions (www.help.senate.gov), the House Committee on Education and the Workforce (www.edworkforce.com), ED's Office of Early Learning (www2.ed.gov/about/offices/list/oese/oel/index.html), and HHS's Office of Early Childhood Development (www.acf.hhs.gov/programs/ecd).

Efficiently Using Meeting Time

DC meetings are short — typically 15–30 minutes for Hill meetings and a bit longer for meetings with Administration staff. Always start by asking the staffer how much time she has. Next, ask if she has heard about your organization, issue, or position before so that you do not waste time reviewing background information your staffer already has. As a rule of thumb, a three- to five-minute introduction is sufficient. The next five to seven minutes should be spent presenting your "Ask" and accompanying materials. Use the remainder of the meeting to discuss follow-up opportunities.

Making Use of Supporting Materials

Good presentations are supported by research and data. Most effective is a one-page, double-spaced summary, which includes a few sentences about your organization, your "Ask" for the meeting, and supporting research or statistics. A short PowerPoint presentation (three to five slides) is also a good way to vary the format. Always offer to email any supporting documentation, including the one-page summary.

Effectively Following Up After Your Meeting

The last few minutes of a meeting should be spent laying the groundwork for follow-up. (Do not forget to exchange business cards.) Similar to scheduling your meeting, the best way to follow up after a meeting is via email. Before you leave, ask your DC staffer if there are staffers in your Senator's or Representative's district offices with whom you should connect, as these are often untapped resources. If you are meeting with Administration staff, you can ask whether there is staff in the regional or state offices that you should meet. You should contact these staff to notify them of events in the local community that they or the Senator/Representative may want to attend or to see if there is anything you can do to help them (e.g. provide statistics or insight into areas that might be affected by your "Ask"). Finally, you should ask your DC staffer if there are staffers in other offices with whom you should meet while you are in DC. Undoubtedly, there are others who are as passionate about early childhood issues as you, and meeting with them while you are still in DC affords a great opportunity to build your advocacy network.

Conclusion

From the perspective of those in Washington, like us who are trying to support child well-being through effective policy, our biggest fear (and frustration) is missing the great idea that is not presented well, or failing to solve the problem because it is not well understood.

It is a very exciting time for the field of early childhood, and your expertise and experience matter now more than ever. With the President proposing an expansion of Pre-Kindergarten funding and new Head Start–Child Care Partnerships; Child Care and Development Block Grant legislation in Congress; and, proposed child care regulations and Head Start competition coming out of DHHS, your voice needs to be heard to ensure that these initiatives meaningfully support children. Being effective when 'taking a meeting' can maximize your impact when working with your representatives in Washington to support our nation's youngest children.

Jeffrey Capizzano

Jeffrey Capizzano is President of the Policy Equity Group, a consulting firm that seeks to empower socially conscious organizations by providing research, advocacy, and consulting support. He is a nationally known advocate and researcher with both private and public sector experience. Most recently, he was a Senior Policy Advisor for Early Childhood Education and Development at the US Department of Health and Human Services. He also worked for seven years at the Urban Institute, a prominent Washington, DC-based think tank, where he conducted policy-related research in the areas of early childhood and K–12 education. Mr. Capizzano's work has informed a number of public policy debates and his research has been featured in *The Washington Post*, National Public Radio, and Brookings Institution reports.

Molly Fishman

Molly Fishman, a Legislative Aide for Senator Michael Bennet of Colorado, focuses on Education and Health Policy. Her work for Mr. Bennet, who serves on both the Senate Health, Education, Labor, and Pensions Committee and the Senate Committee on Finance, has underscored the importance of developing policies that will support our next generation of leaders. Molly received a bachelor's degree in political science with an emphasis in international relations from the University of California, Santa Barbara, where she graduated Phi Beta Kappa.

Getting Legislators Out of the Statehouse and Into Your Program

by Eric Karolak

All of us in the early childhood field have been asked to 'take action' many times to get the attention of state or federal elected officials. You make calls and send letters, participate in action days in your capital city, and you may even meet regularly with the officials who represent you and your community. In Congress and in the states, there are 'champions' for early care and education programs — those who 'get it' and have taken the lead on improving policies and supporting funding. But for the others. . . do you ever get the feeling they don't quite know what you're talking about?

One of the best ways to help state and federal elected officials understand child care and early education in this country is to *show* them. Inviting them to visit a child care program can help them engage in their community.

Connecting Policy and Practice

A site visit moves beyond the fact sheets, numbers, and talking points of a regular meeting. You might be surprised to hear that votes have been changed and policies have moved because someone *showed* these decision-makers what was going on in the community. Someone *showed* them a high-quality program and asked for their support in creating policies that

work. Someone showed them how important child care really is, and asked them to take action.

Mary Beth Salomone, Policy Director at the Early Care and Education Consortium (ECEC), says:

"These are more than a tour. This is an opportunity to show our elected officials what is really going on out there and what they need to do to create and support good policies. This is a chance for program providers to show that they really know best about what parents, children, and their staff need."

This summer, Salomone organized a site-visit campaign among ECEC member centers coast-to-coast. Visits like these help to convey a positive message about child care and communities' needs.

What child care is, and why it is important to our communities, must become something real to them, so that you can explain that more can be done with their support for good policies. Giving legislators the chance to see and interact with children, parents, and teachers can be tremendously valuable.

These visits can be used to convey a broad message about the importance of access to high-quality programs and what it takes to provide high levels of quality. Or, the visits can convey a specific policy "ask" such as strengthening the Child and Adult Care Food Program, making more child care subsidies available to families and more workable for providers, encouraging more opportunities for child care programs in the delivery of state-funded Pre-K initiatives, or any other priority moving through your state or Congress. You can connect the dots between the legislation or idea and the real practice going on every day.

A Teachable Moment

Part of the visit will be, of course, a tour of the program. But this isn't just a walk-through. Think about what you can teach them about the services you provide. Every day you implement the policies set by Congress and the states. You are an expert in how it all really works. You have to recruit and retain the best staff, provide materials and a curriculum, cover your fixed costs, and manage the whole program to meet the rising expectations of parents and public stakeholders. You know what it takes to provide high-quality care. Show them examples of this in your classrooms, in your teachers, in your whole program.

Make sure the visit includes not only observation of programs or activities, but also interactions. These interactions can be the most compelling part of the visit. For example:

■ Use circle time as a way to involve the visiting legislator — suggest that she or he pull up a chair!

■ If appropriate, involve the legislator in snack time or lunch, and to show that this is an important part of learning and development.

■ Ask your legislator if he or she is interested in reading a story to the children.

These are all great photo opportunities, too.

Remember, also, that the purpose of their visit is to gain their support in Congress. You have invited them to your program because there is something

> ### Tips
>
> • Remember that legislators may not be able to give more than an hour for this visit.
>
> • Be sure to pick a day and time that the legislator will see the program in action, with children who are awake!
>
> • Involve the visiting legislator in activities with the children.

you want them to do. Make sure you tell them what that is!

During the August Congressional recess, Chad Dunkley, COO of New Horizon Academy, joined freshman Representative Erik Paulsen (R-MN) on a visit to a child care center in Plymouth, Minnesota. As a new member of Congress, this visit provided Representative Paulsen with a way to build connections with his constituents, and it provided the center staff with a way to request his support in meeting the needs of children, families, and providers. Several visits with other officials took place at New Horizon Academy centers this summer. According to Dunkley:

"We were able to demonstrate what early care and education LOOKS like and that definitely left an impression with the officials and their staff. It also demonstrated that we are the experts about what young children and their families need when it comes to high-quality child care and how important it is that the correct information is available to our elected officials."

Even if you know the official and he or she is a champion, a visit to your program is important. The Childcare Business Coalition of Hawaii invited Representative Mazie Hirono (D-HI) to visit a program while she was in her district this summer. Christina Cox, liaison for the Coalition and president of a multi-site preschool, told us:

"We were delighted that Representative Hirono was able to fit us into her busy schedule. She has been a long-time supporter of quality preschool and we are hopeful that the Congresswoman will support the reauthorization of the Child Care and Development Block Grant, which helps provide families access to child care and aims to improve the quality of that care. Recent cuts in the state-funded Preschool Open Doors subsidy program have greatly reduced the number of low-income families able to attend quality preschool programs."

Welcoming back a long-time champion to visit a local program helps to keep in touch. And with so many voices advocating in the early childhood arena, it's good that they hear from a real provider like you.

Inviting Your State and Federal Legislators to Visit

Find out when your state or federal legislators will be back in town and invite them to visit your program! It's easier than you think. Check out the ECEC Site Visit Toolbox for a guide to an easy-to-plan and successful visit, including template invitation letters and ideas for activities. The Toolbox is available at www.ececonsortium.org.

By visiting an early childhood program, we help Members of Congress to see that:

- high-quality early care and learning programs exist.

- the whole picture of birth-to-five is important.

- play is learning and child care is more than babysitting.

- child care is an important economic activity. Each center is a small business that supports lots of workers — your own staff and your parents.

- teachers, staff, and caregivers need and benefit from supports for training and education.

Eric Karolak

Eric Karolak is Chief Executive Officer of Action for Children, the source for child care and early learning services in central Ohio. Prior to returning to his native Ohio, Dr. Karolak was founding Executive Director of the Early Care and Education Consortium, a public policy alliance of thousands of early learning centers that together enrolled nearly one million children in all 50 states. From 2001 to 2006, he led the National Child Care Information Center, the largest federal clearinghouse focused on child care and early education. He has worked closely with states developing the technical aspects of child care assistance programs, quality rating systems, and partnerships across early childhood programs. He has conducted policy research and fiscal analysis in the areas of child welfare, child care, women's labor force participation, and public housing, and has testified before several state legislatures and both houses of the US Congress.

Engaging with School Districts

by Chad Dunkley and Clare Sanford

For many years, high-quality early childhood providers have quietly done some of the world's most important work. We know that children's earliest teachers have significant impact on their development. But as the eyes of the world have begun to look at and elevate the value of our work, some of us can feel undervalued for the work we've been doing for many decades. As additional public resources are directed towards early education, child care is sometimes disregarded as a quality educational option. There is a perception that the only environments suited to prepare children for school are school districts themselves. Such a lack of respect and misunderstanding frustrates us as professionals, setting up barriers between child care and public schools rather than promoting the program alignment and smooth transitions we know are good for young children.

Our role is to help change that. At New Horizon Academy, we can't expect respect and collaboration to magically appear; we must go out and cultivate it. Relationships with school officials are imperative; what we can learn from each other can result in improved experiences for young children on both sides of the equation. Here we share with you some ideas and strategies we have used to collaborate with school officials.

Saint Paul Public Schools

Our first partnership with a public school program started a decade ago with a Saint Paul Public Schools (SPPS) initiative called Project Early Kindergarten. During the process we were able to visit SPPS Pre-K programs, and they visited ours. Initially, we were both surprised and a bit critical about what we did or did not see in each other's classrooms. Our impression was that the district's program focused so much on literacy that activities designed to help the whole child develop across multiple domains were not highlighted. SPPS thought we had too much going on in our classrooms that could distract from the goal of developing literacy skills. As in any good partnership, we found that we each had things to learn from the other. Working together we enhanced some of our academic skill instruction, and the district increased their understanding of developmentally appropriate practice for young children, namely that children can learn a variety of important skills, including academics, through hands-on experiences. We took our respective areas of expertise and created something greater.

Though Project Early Kindergarten officially ended in 2012, we all felt that ongoing collaboration was not only effective, but crucial to the success of students attending two New Horizon Academy locations in low-income neighborhoods of the city. We have been thrilled to continue a partnership with SPPS at these centers. Now a coach visits each program on a regular basis to:

- observe classrooms and teachers.

- provide support to parents.

- help organize transition activities such as bus rides to local elementary schools for children and parents.

- offer specific instructional strategies so that we are even better aligned with the schools that will be receiving our children.

As Nikole Logan from the SPPS Office of Early Learning states,

"[The SPPS] partnership with several New Horizon locations has been a developing relationship of reciprocal learning and alignment. Increased knowledge of best practices, support with implementation, and awareness of child development have made for more appropriate classroom practices, materials, and decisions about learning. New Horizon Academy teachers say it has been helpful to know more intimately what school districts expect so they know how to better prepare children, and directors indicate that they have more knowledge of how their children are actually transitioning and performing to further inform their center/classroom practices."

Through this collaboration we learned that understanding each other's environment helps everyone improve.

Caring for Kids Initiative

Another partnership is the Caring for Kids Initiative (CfKI) in suburban Wayzata, Minnesota. CfKI is a collective-impact collaboration between a local non-profit (Interfaith Outreach & Community Partners) and Wayzata Public Schools aimed at helping the community's low-income families with young children succeed in both school readiness and family stability. CfKI's unique feature is that it serves what is typically regarded as a wealthy community, one most Minnesotans do not associate with poverty. Its existence serves to support families with low-income, as well as to highlight the varied needs that exist in all communities.

Families choosing to participate in CfKI are offered scholarships to access early education services. Wayzata Public Schools offers a part-time preschool program, and families in need of year-round programs are referred to CfKI's local Quality Provider Network. New Horizon Academy has four centers participating in this network. These providers commit to participating in monthly gatherings to share data and dialogue with District staff to align instruction. In turn they have access to additional resources such as anti-bias curriculum, various trainings, and instructional materials. CfKI works with its partners to provide parent education, a family social worker, and access to intense support in housing, employment, transportation, and basic needs.

The superintendent of Wayzata Public Schools, Dr. Chace Anderson, said after a recent visit to one of New Horizon Academy's CfKI-participating centers,

"It is essential that communities engage cooperatively as they prepare the youngest learners for a positive launch into their K-12 journey. A school district can gain important insights about its educational partners by learning about their programs and services. Working collaboratively improves the likelihood of better prepared children who are destined for a successful learning experience."

Invite Your School Districts

These two projects in St. Paul and Wayzata led us to believe there are more opportunities to build relationships with public schools. So we crafted a letter inviting superintendents to visit our programs. Many superintendents came, and all were impressed with how comprehensive our programs for young children are. In one case a superintendent recommended that her elementary principals and kindergarten teachers tour our programs themselves. After one such visit, school leaders approached us to build a special education partnership at our Maplewood 3M center.

The United States Department of Education recently began identifying excellent, innovative partnerships between public education and private child care providers. New Horizon Academy was the second private program in the country to be highlighted. Our Maplewood 3M center's partnership with Independent School District 622 in suburban St. Paul, Minnesota, was selected for this honor based on its model of inclusion for children with special needs.

District 622 recognized issues faced by families in its early childhood special education program, such as full-day and/or year-round programming, that the district could not provide. After a tour of New Horizon Academy showcased the educational environment a high-quality community child care provider could offer, district staff proposed a unique partnership: they would fund six part-time spaces in New Horizon Academy's preschool rooms, provide on-site support during the hours identified when children were in attendance (with district special education teachers and therapists), and offer joint professional development for both district special education and New Horizon Academy staff. New Horizon Academy gained strategies that benefit all children, not only those with identified disabilities. Adaptations such as rearranged classroom environments and increased print size on labels for child materials were implemented, and in working together in classrooms both New Horizon Academy and District staff learned each other's strategies for enhancing children's social-emotional development, expressive language support, opportunities for active learning, and more.

Director Kari Schmitz reflects on the partnership in saying,

"Not only has [it] provided a wonderful experience for our shared students, but our other children, our staff, and I have benefitted from the resources ISD 622 was able to provide. We learned innovative

strategies for working with children with special needs, additional methods for behavior management, and current information on the assessment and IEP process. It is obvious we all have the same passion for early learning and a desire to see children succeed."

ISD 622 Early Learning Supervisor Ruth Paisley echoes this enthusiasm:

"[We] strive to serve young children in high-quality settings so the partnership with New Horizon Academy was a natural fit with our goals. Our Early Childhood Special Education services were looking for ways to connect families to the community early care and education settings that could provide wrap-around daily care and avoid unnecessary transitions for children. We started small, with six children, and the new partnership in school year 2014-2015 exceeded our expectations. The New Horizon Academy and District staff forged strong collaborative partnerships in serving children and learning through each other's expertise, wrap-around services were provided for children who needed them, and in one situation we were able to serve a child who had not been successfully provided special education services in any other setting."

New Horizon Academy, ISD 622, and parents were so pleased with the partnership's success that the number of children served through special education was significantly expanded for the 2015-2016 school year.

What Child Care Providers Can Do

Start with a letter to your local school district(s). For many the biggest hurdle is the invitation itself, but it need not be overwhelming. Determine what school district(s) your programs are in, and look up the names of the superintendents and Early Childhood Education staff. Compose a short letter that includes some basic information about your program: years in operation, number of children you serve, and any accreditation/certification you hold. Explain that you are proud to prepare children for success in kindergarten and beyond, and that you would like to invite officials to tour your program and explore ways you can collaborate to best serve families and promote successful transitions.

If you invite them, they will come… sometimes. Not every invitation gets a response, and not every tour results in a working collaboration. It's important to remember, however, that every positive interaction between school officials and child care programs builds respect, trust, and contributes to learning on both sides. We need more of these interactions across the country to further elevate our field.

In Conclusion

There are many types of partnerships that can be created that are unique to your programs and school districts. These are just a few examples of the possibilities. And, once you invite school leaders, don't stop there. New Horizon Academy makes it a practice to invite local and state government officials to also visit our classrooms. All of these efforts have taught us that the best way to get respect for the work we do is to take action and bring people in to see our classrooms.

Chad Dunkley

Chad Dunkley is Chief Executive Officer for New Horizon Academy and Kinderberry Hill. He oversees operations, marketing, strategy, and finance, and drives the culture of 'continuous improvement' at all New Horizon and Kinderberry Hill locations. Chad received his J.D. from William Mitchell College of Law and his B.A. in management from Hamline University. Chad is President of the Minnesota Child Care Association (MCCA), on the governing board of National Association for the Education of Young Children (NAEYC), and on the board and executive committee of Early Care and Education Consortium (ECEC).

Clare Sanford

Clare Sanford is Director of Government and Community Relations for New Horizon Academy and Government Relations Chair for the Minnesota Child Care Association. She received her B.A. from St. Olaf College and her Masters in Public Policy from Harvard University's Kennedy School of Government.

3

CHAPTER 3

Promoting Your Program

Marketing: No Longer an Afterthought

by Phyllis Kalifeh

Who would ever have thought that a big white duck quacking AFLAC would be a successful marketing strategy for an insurance company or GEICO's green gecko lizard with a British accent for that matter? Yet marketing and advertising professionals would definitely consider both of these campaigns very successful. What did they have in common besides large advertising budgets and massive television exposure? They were creative approaches for what can be considered rather mundane products, presented in a manner that was both entertaining and eye-catching. Their appeal seems to be universal; yet what we most remember is not exactly the specific message, but the companies they represent.

Relax. I'm not suggesting that those who work in the early childhood field should follow suit and create multi-million dollar campaigns. We know this is not realistic or practical. What we can learn from these examples is that we need to get out of our comfort zones, think outside the box, and address our roles as marketers in a society that is overloaded with information. How can we get the attention of the market segment we're trying to attract?

In a declining economy, it's even more important to consider how we're communicating and marketing our services to our target populations. If you're thinking, "I can't handle one more thing. My plate is full," not a problem, especially if you have all the business you want or need. This article isn't for you. But if you're interested in staying ahead of the game and boosting enrollment, you might want to read on.

Defining Our Terms

You may be thinking, "What's the difference between marketing, advertising, and public relations?" That's a good question and often those terms are muddled. Basically, the end result is to match goods or services to meet the needs of a customer; therefore, advertising and public relations are tools — of a sort — for marketing. To demonstrate, **marketing** is striking up a conversation with another parent in your child's open house at school. During the conversation, you explain how he or she might benefit from a top-notch preschool for the preschooler in tow. You tell them about your school or family child care home, the success of your program, and how it is likely a good option for the parent to consider.

Advertising is when you go up to the parent and confidently talk about how fantastic your school is, hand out a business card or brochure, and share how well your students have done (not divulging confidential information, of course).

Public relations is when a prospective parent comes to you and says, "I've heard great things about your school and would really like to know more about it." Bottom-line is that it's all about the bottom-line, and relationship-building is central to the success of your efforts, regardless of the terminology. We're in the people business, of course!

Back to Basics

First, it's important to get our own houses in order. Good marketing starts with providing the best possible services. The best advertising strategies in the world won't be effective if we can't keep parents because our services are inferior. This is the critical foundation for any successful marketing effort. For example, the building and playground are in good repair, licensing inspections are clean, and children are engaged in developmentally-appropriate readiness activities that promote early learning with responsive nurturing teachers who are well-trained for their jobs. Whew! That's no small order, but fundamental to the success of your marketing efforts. Make sure you've spent the time necessary to lay a solid foundation of high quality for young children. Don't get caught up in the chicken and the egg argument (e.g. "If I had more children enrolled, I could do a better job.") Do the best with what you have now, making the very best decisions possible. If you need to invest more money to get your program up to par, consult a financial advisor and "just do it" (a branding term that Nike coined, by the way, that was also very successful).

Make a Plan

Don't wince! A plan is important, not for the document that you produce, but for the opportunity it presents to think in a systematic way about how you will invest your limited time and resources in marketing your program. The plan is dynamic and provides an internal roadmap. It will also be important as you evaluate the effectiveness of your strategies. Your plan can be as simple or as elaborate as you need, but at a minimum should include about five columns:

■ Your strategies (a description of what you will do)

■ A timeline for when you will undertake that strategy (remembering that marketing is a year-round endeavor)

■ Materials and resources needed to accomplish the strategy

■ A list of who is responsible or tasked with accomplishing the work

■ A description of the costs

■ Optional: You might also want to create a column for evaluating the strategy, determining how you will measure success

Thinking about this in advance will help you refine your plan and adopt the most effective strategies in the future. Making the plan work for you in managing your marketing effort is what's most important.

Tools in the Toolbox

Before we talk about strategies, it's important to think about the tools at your disposal and what you can manage well. For the purpose of framing, we'll organize the tools as follows:

■ Print media (parent handbooks, business cards, brochures, press releases, advertisements, give-aways)

■ Electronic media (website, social networking, email)

■ Staff (an often overlooked marketing resource)

■ Parents (some of your best public relations specialists)

■ Events (employer partnerships, school transition partnerships, open house, Kids' Day, legislative tours, parent appreciation)

Using this frame, it's time to brainstorm potential strategies for your plan.

Print media: This is not a time to scrimp to save a nickel. Your printed materials are a reflection of you and your business. Your image should reflect professionalism. This does not mean that you have to spend a lot of money; you can often garner the help of others to get the professional image you seek. One way to do this is to pay attention to other brochures and print materials that have caught your eye and develop a file of these. What attracts you? Check out the resources in your local community; is there a school or college with a graphic design department? Can you employ the help of students to draft some designs? The content of your materials is as important as their appearance. Be sure that materials are succinct, free of errors, and well written. If you don't feel confident in this area, make sure to have others read and review your materials (possibly parents at your school) to make sure they're reader-friendly, professional, and communicate the message you're trying to convey. Compare prices on printed materials. There are many online printing services in addition to local printing companies in your area. It pays to shop around as prices can vary widely. At a minimum, be sure to have business cards, a brochure, and a parent handbook to share with the public and potential customers.

Consider developing short press releases to publish in the local newspaper, community parent magazine, PTA newsletters, and your own parent newsletter about what's happening at your school. Lengthy news stories will likely be disregarded. Highlighting the implementation of a new curriculum, celebrating a success such as accreditation, the accomplishments of staff, or a visiting celebrity will catch the attention of the public and potential customers (and these are typically free). Make sure to include these stories in your plan.

Electronic media: Some of us have sauntered gently into the technological age and others have come kicking and screaming. Regardless, the age of electronic media is here to stay and getting more sophisticated all the time. If you don't have a website, create one. If you have one, make sure it's current and fresh. There's nothing worse than a website with a posting that's more than a year old! Make sure it's someone's job to keep the website current. Remember, if it's *everyone's* job, it's *no one's* job — so ensure that someone is assigned to the task. If you have a Facebook page for the school, use it! If you don't have one, get one — it's free. It's a great way to post activities, menus, announcements, and accomplishments. If you post pictures of the children, make sure you have parent permission to do so. Some programs have found Twitter to be an effective means of keeping communication lines open. Use the tools at your disposal — you can bet your parents and potential customers are using them! Do you have the email addresses of your parents? Do they use text messaging? These are important resources for managing your day-to-day communications with parents and will help them stay informed. They will boast to their coworkers about how well informed they are about their child's well being, thanks to you!

Staff: Your teaching and support staff can be some of your best ambassadors or your worst nightmare. If staff feels good about where they work, feels a sense of importance in the work they do, believes they're treated fairly and respectfully, then they will sing your praises to existing and potential customers. While we know that funding is limited to pay the types of salaries and benefits we know early childhood teachers deserve, ensure that you do all that you can to provide other incentives (e.g. recognition, rewards, incentives for referrals and enrollments). Build intentional strategies into your marketing plan to support your staff and assume nothing. Personal thank-yous, gift cards, massages, a day off, and small bonuses are some ways that staff knows that they're important to you and the school. There is no substitute for a well-trained, fairly compensated, and appreciated workforce in early childhood — your success is dependent on their success.

Parents: Okay, they're obviously your target market, but have you really thought about how they can be a part of your marketing strategy? Besides word-of-mouth advertisement — which is incredibly important — have you considered referral incentives for your parents such as tuition vouchers for each new paid enrollment, thank-you cards, gift certificates to a nice restaurant? Get creative! Ask your parents what they would like and include their efforts in your marketing plan.

Events: This is typically the area where child care programs feel most confident, but get some mileage out of your events. Invite your legislators to visit your program; provide photo opportunities for them and invite the media (newspaper, radio, and television). If it's a slow news day, the news crew might show up. Develop partnerships with nearby employers: provide tuition or registration fee discounts and advertise your partnerships in company newsletters. Are you a member of your local Chamber of Commerce? If not, consider joining to network with other business owners. Keep your antennae continually attuned to opportunities to leverage your relationships in the community to support your program and the children you serve. Remember, it's a great opportunity for businesses to advertise their community service connections as well.

In Conclusion

It's a new day. Marketing can no longer be an afterthought. It should be incorporated into the psyche of every early childhood program leader. If you offer incredible programs for young children with astounding results and no one knows about it (like the proverbial tree falling in the woods), you may enjoy short-term success that cannot be sustained. To build long-term sustainability, think about how you can make 'marketing' your new best friend. And be creative — remember the lesson of the quacking duck!

Phyllis Kalifeh

Since 2000, Phyllis Kalifeh has led the Children's Forum as its President and CEO. She has executed the strategic plans of the board to improve quality, affordability, and availability of early learning and after-school in the state of Florida through leadership, advocacy, and services to local communities. The Children's Forum also administers the 21st Century Community Learning Centers initiative in partnership with the Florida Department of Education. As one of the leading advocates for children, Kalifeh has obtained millions of dollars in grants, been published countless times, and has presented at nearly 50 conferences and meetings. She serves on the National Registry Alliance Board of Directors, the finance committee for Child Care Aware of America, and board member of Project K.I.D. She received the Excellence Award in School Readiness Program for the Children's Forum Quality Counts Career Center in Miami-Dade County in July 2011. Kalifeh completed her Ed.D. at Florida State University in 2013 with a focus in education policy and evaluation in early education. She holds a Master of Science in Educational Leadership from Florida State, and a Bachelor of Arts in Early Childhood and Elementary Education from the University of West Florida. Phyllis and her husband Steve reside in Tallahassee. They have six sons (three married) and six grandchildren.

Marketing Strategies that Work in Early Childhood Education

by Bruce Schon and Roger Neugebauer

Planning Strategy: Marketing is Not a 4-Letter Word

Marketing is often viewed as a tactic to which no self-respecting early childhood provider would stoop. Certainly anyone who has shopped for a car and experienced the sex-on-wheels ads, the slick sales pitches, and the high-pressure bargaining is aware that marketing practices often are highly objectionable.

Yet, marketing is, in fact, an appropriate, even necessary, activity for early childhood programs. Child care centers must publicize their services so that families who need these services can find them. Additionally, centers that depend upon parents' fees to meet their budgets must actively recruit children to operate at full capacity.

To say that centers need to market their services is not to say that they must engage in slick or high-pressure tactics. This article will attempt to demonstrate that child care programs do have a variety of options available to them in honestly promoting their services. Four guidelines to use in developing a marketing strategy will be outlined, and a number of techniques for implementing this strategy will be described.

Guideline 1. Adapt your marketing approaches to the varying stages of readiness among families in the community. Not all families in your community are equally ready to entrust their children to your center's care. Some are totally unaware of the existence of your program. Others are aware of it, but not especially interested in it. A smaller number are interested in it, but undecided about enrolling their children. Parents, in other words, are in different stages of readiness to sign up for your services. An effective marketing strategy must include specific approaches to families in each of these stages.

Promoting Awareness: Let Them Know You Exist

Guideline 2. Concentrate your publicity where parents needing child care services are most likely to perceive it when they are actively looking for child care or when they are in settings that require them to use child care.

■ **Know your consumers.** Everyone in town doesn't need to know about your center. What matters is that you get the word out to those families who need the services you offer. In order to communicate to these potential users, you first need to identify who they are. One means of identifying your audience is to focus on consumer characteristics. In each of the categories below, identify for whom your services are most appropriate:

- **Parent characteristics** — Working parents, single parents, teenage parents

- **Child characteristics** — Infants, preschoolers, school-age, special needs

- **Program characteristics** — Families seeking caretaking, developmental activities, socializing experiences, readiness activities, health services

- **Operational characteristics** — Families' income levels, home and job location, hours of need, transportation requirements

Hopefully, this process will yield a fairly specific profile (or profiles) of your potential consumers. For example, it might be middle- to upper-income working parent families seeking full-day caretaking and socialization experiences for their preschoolers. Having your audience thus defined, your next task is to make your presence known to them.

■ **Contact referral sources.** Where do parents turn for suggestions when they are looking for child care services? These sources of referral are the most effective points for publicizing your services. An important marketing task, therefore, is to identify the referral sources likely to be used by your potential consumers.

There seldom is a single obvious source for parents to turn to in most communities. Rather, parents utilize a wide range of formal and informal referral sources including: city health departments, welfare agencies, private social and family service organizations, libraries, churches, local employers, women's organizations, unions, licensing agencies, pediatricians, college early childhood departments, elementary schools, parenting classes, child-bearing classes, United Way agencies, local SECA and NAEYC chapters, and other child care programs.

There is no substitute for personal contact as a means of ensuring that referral sources are dutiful in publicizing your program. For example, some directors visit the executives of major employers in the community. They point out how many of their employees are currently benefiting from their center, as well as what services their center can offer employees. If the person at the referral source has met a representative of a center face to face, the likelihood of her remembering and recommending the center is greatly increased. Once personal contact is established, it should be maintained by periodic calls, especially in the form of thanks for referrals made.

■ **Secure free publicity.** A number of avenues are available to directors in pursuing free publicity. The most common means is the issuance of press releases. Press releases should periodically be sent to community newspapers to keep your name before the general public. Additionally, they should also be sent to the newsletters of local unions, businesses, and social service organizations to more directly communicate with potential users.

A second approach is to capitalize on the visibility of your facility. Efforts should be made to make the outward appearances of your building attractive and to prominently display a sign from which passers-by can easily read the center's name, type of services offered, and phone number. Some programs also boldly display the center's name and phone number on their school buses.

Centers should also be alert to the publicity potential of fundraising. In all fundraising activities, whether fairs, sales, or phone solicitations, your center should be clearly identified as the sponsor. Brochures describing your services should be distributed to participants. Representatives should be eager and able to describe your services.

■ **Utilize social networks.** In the past, centers advertised openings in traditional sources such as newspapers and yellow page directories. Today, however, programs need to strut their stuff in social networks. Every center needs to have a Facebook page that presents its story in an attractive and informative way. Online referral sources, such as Craigslist and local variations of this, now must be a basic part of a center's marketing arsenal. If there is a local Resource and Referral service, a center needs to be included on their online platform.

Creating Interest: Communicate Your Strengths

Guideline 3. Identify and emphasize your program's dominant features and marketable differences.

■ **Know your strengths.** To prompt parents who know about your program into seriously considering enrollment for their children, there must be some spark for their interest. They must perceive some unique feature, which causes them initially to select your program from among the various alternatives.

To communicate its dominant features to potential users, a program must first define for itself what these features are. What are the program's strengths? What are its major goals? What aspects of the program are unique? Why should a parent select it as the best place for his or her child?

Examples of dominant features might include curriculum characteristics such as an emphasis on learning through play or enacting school readiness, service characteristics such as strong nature component or 24-hour care, or operational characteristics such as a highly trained and skilled staff or a sliding scale for fees.

■ **Clarify your image.** Having defined your major strengths, it is necessary to communicate them to potential users. The most direct approach is to make the center's dominant features a central theme in all promotional activities. In the long run, however, it is also vital to concentrate on establishing a public image based on these features.

Although Madison Avenue tends to act as if public image can be created overnight, a more realistic view is that…

"an organization is not a chameleon capable of acquiring any desired image…. One does not acquire an image simply through public relations planning. The image is largely a function of the actual deeds of the organization." (Kotler)

If a child care center wants to convey an image of providing 'comprehensive developmental services,' for example, it must, in fact, be providing 'comprehensive developmental services.' If a center is unable to deliver on its promises for quality of care, no amount of public relations will establish a positive public image. On the other hand, if a program's performance is as high as its pronounced standards, there are a number of techniques available for supporting the communication of a positive image.

■ **Promote personal recommendations.** In child care, the great majority of children are recruited by word-of-mouth. Potential users of services are most influenced by recommendations from their friends who use the services because the method of delivering the endorsement is personal and the source of the endorsement is known and trusted.

Given the prime importance of word-of-mouth, a director might do well to encourage and influence the flow of personal recommendations. The director should tell parents that their spreading the word is very beneficial to the program and is most appreciated. Some centers even offer parents who recruit another family a discount on their fee.

In addition, the director should provide similar encouragement to other center representatives. Teachers, board members, volunteers, and parents of preschool alumni all come into contact with potential users in their lives outside the center. The director should identify and encourage all such potential promoters.

In encouraging all of these informal representatives of the center, the director might find it beneficial to remind them of the dominant features of the center. A one-page fact sheet listing the program's goals and strengths, services, and enrollment requirements might be distributed as a resource to those likely to spread the word.

■ **Establish your reputation.** A center's reputation for providing quality early childhood services can be communicated more widely if the center provides other services to families with young children. Families not currently in the market for child care have many other child-related needs. By helping meet these needs, your center can strengthen its image in the community of being a reliable and caring resource for parents and children. Examples of such services include:

  • **Parenting workshops.** Ongoing or one-shot workshops could be offered to parents to provide practical advice on a wide range of problems they encounter in raising children. Topics could include first aid with children, dealing with aggression, developing self-image and independence, discipline problems, sex issues, talking with children, or designing children's rooms.

  • **Babysitting referral.** The center could screen and train babysitters and charge them an initial fee to be listed. Parents needing babysitting would then pay an initial registration fee to be able to call in for recommendations on sitters.

  • **Newspaper column.** An arrangement could be made with the local newspaper whereby the center would provide a regular column on practical advice to parents on child-rearing or children's activities.

  • **How-to pamphlets.** A two- to four-page pamphlet could be designed and written by the center on how to select children's books, with selection pointers as well as an annotated list of recommended books for children at different age levels. Similar pamphlets could focus on selecting children's toys, designing children's rooms, engaging in creative play, or dealing with behavior problems. Pamphlets could be advertised in the local paper or over the radio and distributed widely through pediatricians, churches, libraries, and service clubs. Those on books and

toys could be promoted most effectively prior to the holidays.

  • **Children's activities.** Once a week, classes for children could be offered in creative movement, gymnastics, or swimming. A children's entertainment series with puppet shows, plays, or films could be provided on Saturday mornings.

Two final pointers: First, select services that not only are needed in the community, but also are challenging to your staff. These services should provide a stimulating outlet for the talents of your staff, as well as a refreshing change of pace for them. Second, be sure to get proper credit for your center. In any of these services, clearly identify your center as the sponsor, and briefly describe your services and outstanding features.

Securing Commitments: Consider the Parents' Needs

Guideline 4: Make doing business with you an easy and pleasant experience for parents.

When you have succeeded in interesting parents in your center, you should be able to convert this interest into a commitment if you can meet their two primary needs at this stage of readiness. First and foremost, they will need to be assured that your center is a reliable place to leave their child. Typically, the most important factors for parents in selecting a child care center or nursery school are:

■ well-trained staff.

■ warm and loving caregivers.

■ clean and safe environment.

In the parents' initial contacts with the center, therefore, you should be especially careful to satisfy their concerns about the staff and the environment.

Keep in mind that your program cannot be all things to all families. If your program's philosophy is 'learning through play,' and parents approach you wanting their children to get an early start on academics, this may not be a good match. You might attempt to persuade these parents that learning through play is, in the long run, the best way to prepare children for academic success. But if, in the end, a parent insists on wanting something you cannot provide, do not bend your values just to gain another enrollment.

Second, you should be alert to the fact that in initiating contact with your center parents may well experience the uneasiness and uncertainty of entering a new situation. You should take steps in the early stages of contact to put the parent at ease. If you make parents anxious and frustrated in doing business with you, they may well choose not to do business with you at all.

■ **Improve phone contact.** The manner in which a parent's initial inquiry, usually in the form of a phone call, is handled will often be a major factor in shaping his opinion of the center. No matter how wonderful a center is, if it creates a disinterested, disorganized, or bureaucratic impression in the initial phone call, chances are it will be eliminated from consideration by that parent. The following suggestions, along with a heavy dose of courtesy, might be helpful in overcoming early turn-off:

• Be specific in describing your program. State your goals and strengths in more than stereotyped generalities. Outline how your staff is qualified to achieve your goals.

• Be clear in describing the admissions process.

• Let them know that you are sensitive to the specific concerns parents have about their own children.

• Encourage them to visit the center. Without exerting pressure, try to set up a time for a visit.

• Offer to provide them names of parents who have used the center and who can be called for reactions.

■ **Quickly respond to online inquiries.** Parents initiating inquiries online is becoming more and more common. On your website you should include a brief survey form for parents to complete in making the inquiry. This form should ask for basic information about the child, the types of service they want (part-time, full-time), and what their educational goals would be. If they contact your center by email, call them if they include a phone number, and if not, link them to the survey for making a formal inquiry. Today people expect instant answers to their online messages, so do not delay in responding.

■ **Facilitate observations.** The moment of highest anxiety for parents is when they come to observe your program. Entering a room of unknown children and adults without a clear role to play can make a parent observer feel quite awkward: Should I sit or stand? Should I play with the children? Should I talk to the teachers? How and when should I leave?

Centers can help eliminate much of this anxiety with a few simple procedures:

• When prospective parents schedule visits, they should be sent a description of the program, as well as a list of suggestions on what they might do and look for in their observations.

• When parents arrive at the center, there should be someone ready to greet them by name. The greeter should give them a tour of the facility, provide a brief description of the classroom structure for the room in which they will observe, review the pointers on observing, and answer any last-minute questions.

• In bringing parents into the classroom, the greeter should introduce them to the teachers and to the children.

• At some point during observations, the head teacher should come over to explain what activities are going on.

- Parents could be invited to bring their child to participate in classroom activities while the parent observes. This can be reassuring to parents if the teachers are skilled at easing a child into a new situation.

- Thought should also be given to the effect the environment has on parents when they first enter the center. If their immediate impression is of shabbiness or carelessness, the likelihood of their being impressed with the center's positive features will be lessened considerably.

■ **Sharpen interview techniques.** Many parents also request an in-person interview with the director to clear up any final areas of uncertainty. Directors find that the following ideas make for the most effective interviews:

- An informal format is best — opening with the parents' questions and closing with the director's explanation of enrollment procedures and operating policies.

- Some directors find it beneficial to discuss parents' perceptions based on their observations. Other directors like to discuss the needs of the child and how the program would deal with these needs. It may be reassuring to discuss the background and skills of the teachers, as well as to offer the teachers' résumés for review.

- If finances are a problem, the director might offer to explore parents' potential eligibility for public subsidies or private scholarships. If these do not apply, the 20% rebate under the tax credit should be explained.

- The bottom-line, once the parent has been moved from awareness to interest to the point of making a decision, is that this final decision will be based on the quality and appropriateness of the program in the eyes of the parent. If a program's quality is low, parents will not decide to sign up — no matter how effective its marketing is. On the other hand, if quality is high, an effective marketing strategy will provide for stable growth for the center and informed decision making by the parents.

Helpful Resources

"Building Enrollment." (2011). *VOICES: Insights from the Field.* Redmond, WA: Exchange Press.

Copeland, T. (2009). *Family child care business planning guide.* St. Paul, MN: Redleaf Press.

Kotler, P. (1975). *Marketing for nonprofit organizations.* Englewood Cliffs, NJ: Prentice-Hall, Inc.

Macarthy, A. (2014). *500 social media marketing tips.* www.andrewmacarthy.com

"Strategies for Promoting Your Program." (2013). *Exchange Essentials.* Redmond, WA: Exchange Press.

Wassom, J. (2010). *Basic techniques for securing enrollment: Updated edition.* Denver, CO: The Julian Group, Inc.

Wassom, J. (2009). *Keys to marketing a professional image.* Denver, CO: The Julian Group, Inc.

Bruce Schon

Bruce Schon is a consultant to *Exchange Magazine.*

Roger Neugebauer

Roger Neugebauer is founding publisher of *Exchange Magazine* and a co-founder of the World Forum Foundation.

SCOPE is Marketing

"Good Management Begins with Good People"

by Dennis Vicars

As many of you know, from prior writings and personal friendships, the idea of SCOPE (Safe, Clean, Organized, Professional, Educational) came to me in the mid-'80s after watching numerous focus groups with parents discussing what was important to them and what their priorities were for a positive early care and education experience. It's safe to say that if we keep these five priorities as the centerpiece of our daily operation and don't get bogged down in the competing challenges that come our way, we will have well-run programs that are consistent with parents' values.

SCOPE, however, goes much further than the priorities of operating a well-run, operationally effective center. It can also be used as the foundation, both internally and externally, for marketing a high-quality early care and education environment. If everything we do is marketing (and it is), then running a good operation through the priorities of SCOPE automatically lends itself to marketing the best of what we do on a daily basis.

Safe

We all understand that safety is the single most important part of operating a high-quality program. However, have you ever stopped to think about how the safety of your center impacts marketing? Safety is the number one priority for families who tour your center. If a family perceives the center as unsafe, they will not enroll their child. If a touring parent sees your center as a safe environment, she will be more likely to enroll — as long as the rest of SCOPE is seen in action throughout the tour as well. Safety weighs heavily on the minds of your current families as well and is assessed daily. A safe center adds to parents' satisfaction which, in turn, increases the rate of retention.

Some marketing ideas built around safety:

■ Host a Health and Safety Fair at the center. Invite your local fire and police departments to provide information for families on a variety of safety issues.

■ Have one of your teachers become state certified in car seat installation and communicate this achievement to families.

■ Ensure that all of your teachers are certified in first aid and CPR, even if your state doesn't require it. Make sure parents know that all staff have completed this training.

■ Bring in the Red Cross to conduct an infant and child CPR and/or first aid training for parents. Publicize the event to enrolled families and the community. If you offer the training outside of center hours, offer child care for families who participate.

■ Bring in an expert on child safety to talk to parents about how to keep their homes and children safe. Offer the event to both enrolled and non-enrolled families. Offer child care if the course is held outside of center hours.

Clean

Like safety, cleanliness has a huge impact on all parents, both those you hope to enroll and the ones you hope to retain. A clean center equates with quality in many parents' minds. As the director of the program, your job is to tell your cleaning staff what clean looks and smells like. Cleaning as you go is a good rule for teachers, staff, and children throughout the day.

Some marketing ideas for cleanliness:

■ Each morning, make sure the parking lot and entranceways are clean of trash and debris and that sidewalks are clear of leaves and mulch. During the summer, ensure that your plants/flowers are watered and any dead plants/leaves are removed.

■ Assign a different teacher each month to help organize and clean the lobby area. Ask these teachers to look at the lobby from a prospective parent's point of view and remove any clutter or items that don't belong there.

■ Each morning, ensure that every room in the building smells fresh. Parents will notice foul odors in the classrooms when they drop off and pick up their children.

■ Bathrooms for parents' use should be inspected every day before and after pick-up and drop-off times for cleanliness and adequate supplies.

■ Keep cleaning supplies accessible to the front desk staff and use these throughout the day to keep the glass of the front door sparkling.

■ Assign a different classroom each week for picking up any garbage from the common areas and the playground at the end of their outside play times, teaching staff and children to take pride in their environment.

■ Ask a trusted parent for an honest perspective on the cleanliness of the building and follow through on his recommendations for improvement.

Organized

ECE professionals are pack rats by nature. We throw out nothing and believe that someday we will use everything we keep. All too often we allow these materials to creep out of the shelves, closets, bookshelves, boxes, and cubbies making our rooms and offices look like the neighborhood yard sale. To a parent's eye, we look disorganized.

Organization affects our marketing effort because parental opinions are formed by their first impressions of our programs and classrooms — and second chances are rarely given. If you can't find a tour packet, or are unprepared for their visit, they may think, "If they can't find paperwork, how are they going to keep track of my child?" Your level of organization has a huge impact on prospective families.

Try these marketing ideas for organization:

■ Ask each teacher to clean and organize their teacher cabinets, closets, and shelves and maintain these on a regular basis.

■ Ask a teacher to clean and organize the supply closet. Rotate the teacher each month, or as often as necessary.

■ Clean and organize the front desk area. The management team needs to be organized, too.

■ Walk through the classrooms. Partner with the teachers in each classroom to identify areas that can be de-cluttered. Take a before picture. Give teachers a couple of days to de-clutter the area, then take an after photo to show them the progress they've made. Do this in each classroom.

■ Walk into your office as a parent would and look at it with a fresh set of eyes. What do you see? Is it clean and organized? If not, put time on your calendar each day for the next five days to clean off your desk; organize bookshelves; dust your desk, cabinets, and lamps; and clean your computer.

Professional

All parents expect that the people who are caring for and educating their children are professionals. Education, experience, maturity, speech, writing ability, character, friendliness, kindness, and the ability to express oneself clearly with confidence are all elements of professionalism in our field. The key to success in ECE is the child-parent-teacher dynamic. When your center staff present themselves to parents in a professional manner, the level of mutual respect increases, as does parental confidence, satisfaction, and retention.

A few marketing ideas for professionalism:

■ Take a day to talk about the center's dress code with each teacher individually. They should fully understand what attire is appropriate for the workplace.

■ Every center has a teacher who is known for being wonderful with parents. Ask this teacher if they are willing to share their ideas about how to communicate with parents with other teachers, with a focus on professionalism.

■ Hold a staff meeting with a professionalism theme. Role play with teachers using real scenarios where professionalism was lacking and discuss how professionalism could have made a difference in the outcome.

■ Give teachers MVP (Most Valuable Professional) awards based on observed professionalism with parents or coworkers.

■ Use spell check before sending out emails, newsletters, and other communications to parents, and encourage staff to do the same.

■ Prepare for scheduled tours by having tour packets already collated. Ensure that you are staffed appropriately so that you are not interrupted during your tour.

■ As the director, you should know the names of every parent and child in your center. You should have the same expectation for your staff.

Educational

Sometimes we get so caught up in our own ECE speak that we forget to view our programs from a parent's perspective. If the child-parent-teacher dynamic is to work, then we need to help parents understand that what might appear at times like 'organized chaos' is early learning at its best.
The more we develop parents' understanding of high-quality programs, the more positively our programs will be perceived. What we do every day to care for and educate children is not always obvious to a parent. It's our job as professionals to help them understand and join us.

These educational marketing tips might help:

■ Each week, browse the web for parent articles. Find out what it is your parents are interested in or focus on a topic that is relevant to what is happening within the center. The director must be the educational leader of the center.

■ Make sure that the 'evidence of learning' is prominent in each classroom. Each class should have at least one board that includes the children's projects, pictures of the children during project creation, a written description of the project, and what the children were learning while creating the project. These should be changed out at least monthly.

- Ensure that the daily schedule is posted along with the most current lesson plan in each classroom.

- Every classroom should be displaying a "What We Did Today" explanation so that parents can see what their children learned throughout the day. This also serves as a prompt for parent-child conversations at pick-up time.

- Include a list of children's learning milestones in your parent newsletter. Help parents understand what to look for and how to participate in developmentally appropriate activities to foster their children's growth.

- Walk through your classrooms and staff break room to ensure that all words are spelled correctly on printed materials. Ask all of your teachers to have a second set of eyes proofread the information on their parent boards prior to posting so that any typos or incorrectly spelled words are corrected before they are displayed.

Superior operations and marketing efforts are inseparable in early care and education. Present and prospective parents assess us every day on what they see, smell, hear, and therefore believe to be a positive environment for their child. Let SCOPE be your operational/marketing foundation.

Dennis Vicars

Dennis Vicars is the President of The Arista Group, Inc. In his career, Dennis has served as a child care corporate executive, preschool company founder, and advocate on both the public and private side of early childhood education. Dennis is past President of the Child Development Policy Institute (CDPI) and a former member of California's Early Learning Advisory Committee (ELAC).

Five Smart Marketing Moves to Build Enrollment

by Julie Wassom

Building enrollment is not as easy as it used to be. Higher parent expectations, more competition, and the incredible power of reviews have made it essential that early care and education managers and administrators understand what I call "The Four Rights of Effective Marketing." For your marketing to be most successful in generating inquiries from qualified enrollment prospects, it must be the...

■ *right message* to the

■ *right target audiences* at the

■ *right time* through the

■ *right venues.*

Assuming who your target audiences are and where they come from is not good enough. Knowing very clearly who and where they are — demographics, psychographics (lifestyles), and geography — will help you know what kind of message will appeal to them and where to put it. For example, working parents will respond to a different message than stay-at-home moms. Parents who jog to the center pushing a runner's stroller will have different life-styles — and thus child care needs — than parents who quickly drive up, drop off their children, and head for the train to their city jobs.

Understanding when prospects are most likely to notice your marketing messages and where they will look for them (venues) can be the difference between a successful marketing campaign and one that yields far fewer inquiries than you had hoped. A campaign timed when parents are seeking to register for the school year will attract more attention than one released at a traditionally less decisive time of year.

Should you allocate your marketing resources to search-engine optimization or to ads in the local parenting magazines or to generating publicity? How do you figure this out? A very good start is to ask this question of every parent who contacts you: "What are the ways you heard about us?" Track their responses, and you will soon have an idea of the best venues for your marketing messages.

When I ask directors what ways their prospects heard about them, most who track it say word-of-mouth is still the most common. However, today's parents are extremely tech savvy. Some sources indicate that over 75% of millennials have a mobile device nearby at all times. This alone begs the question, "If they pay more attention to online marketing than traditional methods, shouldn't your marketing move beyond relying on word-of-mouth to creating what I once heard industry tech expert, Chip Donohue, call *word-of mouse*?"

So what matters in your marketing program? Listed are five smart marketing moves that will give you a measurable return on your investment.

Do a website marketing audit. *Conversion-centered landing page design* is an Internet marketing term that indicates the ability of a website to create experiences that guide the visitor toward completing a specific action. In early childhood education, that action is to convert from website visitors to enrollment prospects. Many ECE sites provide a lot of information, yet do very little to call the web visitor to action. What should that action be? If you want your site to be a strong marketing tool, the action should be for the visitor to request more information or to schedule a center visit. Does your website make it easy and obvious for the prospect to do that?

Take a look at your website from the prospects' perspective:

■ Is it mobile friendly?

■ Is it easy to navigate?

■ Is it visually appealing enough to keep them there?

■ Does it create urgency?

■ Does it have design elements that lead them to the desired action without too many click-throughs?

Make immediate, personalized follow-up part of your protocol. When today's prospects inquire, they expect an immediate response that provides the requested information. The more personalized the response, the better. For inquiries submitted from your website, a response by the end of the business day says to the prospect, "You matter, and I want to help you with this important decision for your child and family." In the work I have done researching parents' perspective on optimal response times, I have learned that if you wait much more than 24 hours to get back to enrollment prospects, you have lost them to one of your competitors.

If you are using an inquiry form or prospect profile, whether a printed version or one prospects have submitted online from your website, the form should include a section where you can request the prospect's specific interests, needs, and concerns. With this information, you can then personalize your follow-up beyond child's age, classroom, and days needed. You can briefly indicate features of your center that will meet parents' expressed needs. As parents proceed from initial investigation to consideration, this personal attention can be a deciding factor that can put you on their short list of centers to visit.

Develop a strong parent referral program. Parents referring other parents remains a significant source of inquiries for most centers. Do an analysis of where your parents are getting referrals. Is it solely by talking face-to-face with other parents? Probably not. In addition, they are reading online reviews, checking licensing websites, asking their pediatricians, and talking to staff. What are you doing to request, promote, acknowledge, and thank referrals in each of these categories of opinion influencers?

If you do not already have a parent referral program, now is the time to develop one. Ask your current parents what would be the most valuable thank-you gift. For many, it is a tuition credit for both the referring family and new family, after a certain period of enrollment. For others it is something else the parent values, such as tickets to a local amusement park or a monthly pass on local mass transit. Once established, promote this program to existing families in your newsletters, on special reminder cards, on your website, and in conversation.

Include staff in your enrollment referral program. They can be valuable sources for new prospects. Develop partnerships in your community where you cross-refer, such as with pediatricians, children's dentists, and hairdressers, to name a few. For these opinion influencers, gift cards and personal thank-you notes can help keep the stream of referrals coming. Without a strong parent referral program, you are missing out on a smart, low-cost marketing opportunity.

Make your email marketing content rich. Just because young parents prefer to communicate via email does not mean they will read every one you send them. However, if you begin to use content marketing in those messages, they will start to recognize them as containing information of value. Value in making this important family decision, value in engaging in your school and with other families there, value in being a better parent. It is then that you will capture their attention and their inquiries.

Though adding a new prospect to the event notices you send other parents is a nice gesture of invitation, it is not content marketing. Sending a link to an article about separation anxiety to a prospective parent concerned about leaving her child is content the parent will see as personal and valuable.

Larger scale email campaigns must attract attention, be well-branded, hold readers long enough to communicate key messages, and give qualified prospects an incentive to respond. If your email marketing supports your position as the knowledgeable, helpful, professional resource your prospects can trust, they will be more likely to inquire to determine what your center's environment feels like for their child and family.

Use a customer relationship management system (CRM) to track prospects from inquiry to registration and enrollment. This marketing tool can also help assess strengths and challenges in the conversion pipeline, and manage the effectiveness of marketing campaigns. For many directors, the task of tracking inquiries and following up is still being done on Post-it Notes® or in a spiral notebook or lead log. Far more efficient and cost-effective is to use available software to make this task easier and the center more competitive in attracting and retaining prospects in the search process.

Fortunately, owners and managers in the child care field can now choose web-based CRM software systems that are both customized to the industry and will integrate into several of the most commonly used management software programs. The reports a good CRM system generates can give small to large ECE companies valuable information for avoiding enrollment prospect loss, developing conversion training, determining lifetime value of customers, and achieving higher rates of return on marketing campaigns.

Conclusion

Smart marketing, like the actions above, will not only generate more qualified inquiries for your center, it will help make enrollment building a more comfortable, easy-to-manage, and yes, even fun part of everyday life in your center.

Julie Wassom

Julie Wassom is a professional speaker and consultant who has helped thousands of directors and managers build significant enrollment in their early care and education programs. An internationally recognized authority on marketing child care services, Julie is president of The Julian Group, Inc., a training and consulting firm specializing in the early care and education industry. She is the author of *The Enrollment Building Success Library* of training resources, and the free online newsletter, *Wassom's Child Care Marketing Wisdom*. Julie can be reached at (303) 693-2306, julie@juliewassom.com, or www.juliewassom.com.

Who Cares?

Eight Principles for Dealing with Customers

by William H. Franklin

Every workday when the doors are unlocked and the lights are turned on, employees take over the real control of this country's businesses.

People who are put off by the way your employees look or the way your place looks aren't coming back, because they're out of their comfort zone.

Your customers can buy their products and services from anyone, but they choose to do business with you. Recently I was in a bookstore, which is a part of a national retail book chain. I couldn't locate the book title I wanted, so I went to the 'customer service' counter — at least that was what was printed on the sign hanging above the attendant's head. Scrolling through the computer catalog, he located the title. "We're out of it," the attendant said. After several seconds of ensuing silence, it became apparent to me that the attendant had concluded our brief encounter — in fact, he had left the counter to do something else. After all, I suppose, I was the one who wanted the book, not him.

Thumbing through the family mail recently, I came upon an important looking letter from a prestigious firm addressed to me — William H. Franklin. I opened and read the letter. It described a variety of financial services the firm could provide if I chose to become their client. Unfortunately, the letter began, "Dear Mr. Williams," evidence that the writer had signed the letter without reading it. I concluded that if the writer couldn't get my name right, he probably couldn't keep my account straight either. So the letter was routed to the trashcan.

It should be a bit unsettling to business managers on hearing tales like these to realize that, as a practical matter, they don't run their businesses — their employees do; these examples prove it. When I buy a meal, rent a car, or search for a book, I don't deal with the company's president, or its manager, or its stockholders; I deal with an employee. And the employee determines the service level I will receive. Every workday when the doors are unlocked and the lights are turned on, employees take over the real control of this country's businesses.

But in a private enterprise economy, like ours, there are choices. And the customer, as the expression goes, is king. Customers ultimately determine which businesses will prosper and which will fail. A large part of that determination is the way they are treated. And when customers are treated badly, they usually don't get mad. They just don't come back. And their business goes to our competitor, probably permanently.

Principle 1
Customers buy solutions — not products or services.

Obviously, when someone has a problem, he wants it solved. I think too many selling situations overlook this fact.

Regardless of the way you promote your business, whether through advertising or direct selling, you raise the expectations of potential customers by what you say that you or your product will do for them. The customer buys the expectation of a solved problem and the benefits of the solution. For example, I don't really buy gas as much as I buy the right to continue to drive my car — and get to where I'm going. Gas is the solution that enables me to do both. I don't really buy a suit of clothes as much as I buy an image, nor do I buy a quarter-inch drill bit as much as I buy a quarter-inch hole. A fine meal in a five-star restaurant should be an experience. I can eat at home.

Better customer service will occur when employees understand that they are in the problem-solving business. If the employee follows all the rules and the customer's problem doesn't get solved, it's a 'no sale,' even though money changed hands. Employees mustn't forget that their expertise is on the line when they are in front of a customer — and that's the business you're really in.

Principle 2
Ask questions.

If customers buy solutions, you must understand the problem to be solved. The difference between selling something and taking an order for it is who does the problem research.

Asking questions minimizes the chance of making a mistake that could later result in a frustrated customer, who may or may not come back to allow you to sort it out. Asking questions is clearly an important selling technique. It demonstrates interest and concern. From the standpoint of rendering customer service, it's important because it singles the customer out to be treated in a special way. A question as mundane as "Smoking or non-smoking?" at a restaurant indicates that there is some concern for a diner's comfort during a meal.

Several years ago I was shopping for a pair of binoculars. The clerk who was waiting on me began putting every model of the binoculars in the display case on the sales counter without a word. Apparently he thought I would make my choice based on weight and color. "Look," I said, "I don't know anything about these things, tell me something about them." Well, this guy had a sales IQ in the single digits because he said, "I really don't know binoculars, I usually work in cameras." I turned to leave, but another clerk, who happened to be waiting on a customer nearby and had overhead the conversation, interrupted and said, "Excuse me, sir, how were you planning to use the binoculars?" "To watch football games," I said. "Then this pair is what you need." The sale was made —but just barely.

Principle 3
Build relationships.

Use the customer's name where it is appropriate, and give yours too. Recently, I took my wife to an upscale restaurant to celebrate our wedding anniversary. After being seated, our waiter approached the table and said, "Mr. Franklin, welcome to 103 West… my name is David, I will be in charge of your service tonight, and let me also introduce you to John and Marcos who will be assisting me." Each time he approached the table, he used my name again. I've dined at many five-star restaurants all over this country, and I'm used to first-class service. But somehow the waiter's tasteful use and reuse of my name when addressing me personalized the service in a way that made us feel that we weren't just one of several tables David was assigned to serve.

How do your employees look? How do they sound on the phone? Does your correspondence read like a canned speech? — or worse still, like stilted bureaucratese? How does your place look? All of these are important elements in developing lasting relationships with customers. People who are put off by the way your employees look or the way your place looks aren't coming back, because they're out of their comfort zone.

Principle 4
If you can't solve a customer's problem, at least say what you can do.

Don't say, "I'm sorry, we're out of that book" (in other words, you have a problem, friend). Say, "We don't have a copy in stock, but I can check our other stores for you." At least the second approach indicates the clerk doesn't have the book, but he does have the problem to solve. So the customer can now let go of the problem. Nothing is more irritating than a mindless robot who in essence says, "I'm sorry, but I can't help you… period."

Principle 5
If a customer must be referred to someone else, at least have the courtesy to stay with the customer until the connection with the other party is made.

This is true whether it is on the telephone or in person. Take the responsibility to run interference through your company's bureaucracy and make sure there is a clean handoff to the next person. Too many times, customers are told they must take the initiative to wander around without help to find the right department or the right person or the right telephone number they need to call.

For example, don't say, "I'm sorry that's not my department — you'll have to call…." Instead say, "Let me take you to Mrs. Harris to introduce you…." Then, before leaving the person with Mrs. Harris, ask them, "Is there anything else I can help you with before I leave you?" You have done your job, and by that last question, you demonstrated that to your customer.

Principle 6
If customers are angry, there's a reason. Deal with the reason, not their anger.

Most customers prepare themselves to receive an insensitive, bureaucratic response to their problems. Anger can often be defused with sympathy. "I don't blame you for being angry that the dress doesn't fit…. Let's see what I can do about it for you."

In other words, focus on discovering a solution with a customer. In the customer's mind, the two of you are on opposite sides of the problem. You must convince that customer that you have come over to the 'other side.'

Principle 7
The resolution of a customer complaint begins with an agreement on a course of action — not an action itself.

As I've just said, most problems arising out of botched customer treatment involve emotions. These must be dealt with first. Consider this: "Why don't you leave your car here and we'll look at it?" How much better it would be to say, "You may be right in suspecting that your front-end is out of alignment, but it could be caused by your tires…. Let's switch the tires to see if the car pulls in the opposite direction…. That won't take but a minute and is less expensive than putting the car on the alignment rack…. Would that be agreeable to you, Mr. Clark?"

When a customer has gotten what he didn't want (the wrong suit, the wrong rental car, no book, or an incorrectly addressed letter), it's reasonable for him to expect he is not going to get his problem resolved either. After all, the person who has goofed it up can't be relied on to straighten it out. Moreover, a wronged customer feels powerless to bring about the necessary corrective action. Getting an agreement before acting is both symbolic and practical. It is symbolic because the customer is invited to participate in identifying corrective action. It is practical because it avoids doing something — even something that would work — that the customer isn't convinced will be satisfactory.

Principle 8
Do something more than the customer expects, then be sure that the customer knows it!

Recently my wife took her car in for the third time to have the mechanic do something about its squealing brakes. Nothing could be found wrong. She refused to accept the car back. The service supervisor concluded the problem was the brake rotors. The conversation went something like this: "Mrs. Franklin, your brake rotors are thin; the manufacturer doesn't recommend turning them. We'd like to replace them and will do it for our parts cost only, if you are willing to leave your car with us tonight. Can someone pick you up and bring you back tomorrow?" They did more than expected, despite the return trips she had made to resolve the problem. And they were willing to lose money to make things right. After all, they were the brake experts, not she.

I've said on many occasions that customers have an internal accounting system. They view a purchase as a favor. After all, your customers can buy their products and services from anyone, but they choose to do business with you. Whether you conducted the business transaction correctly or incorrectly, customers now view the purchase as a favor, as a 'credit,' and they 'debit' your side of the ledger so that you are always working your way out of a deficit condition with customers. This shop did a good job of breaking even in the only way it counts to a customer.

When you or one of your employees has fouled something up, you really owe the customer — big time. So it is essential that you not only correct a problem, but also you must be willing to lose money to set things straight. If Federal Express, for example, fails to deliver by 10:30 am, the service is free. They didn't do what they promised: "Absolutely, Positively, Overnight." I recently took my daughter to a very nice restaurant to celebrate her thirteenth birthday. The service was slow, and the waiter had reduced my bill before he handed it to me. And he told me why

it was reduced. Just like the mechanic's approach — "We'll switch your front tires to see if the car pulls then in the opposite direction, and we'll do that at no charge to you…. How does that sound?" It sounds like a winner talking!

This article was adapted, with permission from the publisher, from William Franklin's book, *Street Smarts: New Ideas for Small Companies* (1990). To order a copy send $24.95 to the Georgia State University Business Press, College of Business Administration, Atlanta, GA 30303-3093, or call (404) 651-4253.

William H. Franklin

William H. Franklin is a consultant to entrepreneurs of small- to mid-sized companies. He speaks frequently to associations of owners of privately held companies, and he is the author of books and articles that address small business management issues. He is on the faculty of Georgia State University in Atlanta, where he specializes in entrepreneurship and small business development.

Retail 101

What Programs Can Learn from Retail Stores

by Frances Carlson

In my job as a college instructor, I help early childhood teachers plan and implement optimal learning environments for children. To help them focus on what children need in their environments, I ask students to tell me what it is about their favorite store that makes it their favorite: how it feels, how it's organized, what the salespeople are like. I help them understand that children's environments should allow them to feel the same joy and excitement. In reflecting on my students' comments, as well as my own shopping experiences over the years, I've discovered ten tricks from the retail world that help guide us as we establish environments for our children:

Know your customers' names and say them often, in a positive context. When I pay by check or credit card, cashiers often take advantage of my payment method to learn my name. When giving me my receipt, they will say, "Thank you, Ms. Carlson. Have a good day!" I use my pharmacy for one specific reason, and it is not because their prices are lower. I use it because everyone who works there knows my name. As soon as I walk up to the counter, the pharmacist or one of the techs always greets me with, "Hey, Ms. Carlson! What can I help you with today?" And television fans from the '80s will remember a line from the theme song from the popular television show *"Cheers"*: You wanna be where everybody knows your name.

Children love to hear their names. When a teacher says a child's name, the child feels the same sense of acknowledgement and affirmation that we do. That is why teachers must use a child's name often, but in a positive context. Since hearing our names spoken can be so affirming, using a child's name when correcting or redirecting him can make the correction feel like praise. Use children's names to call attention to accomplishments, for example, when a child is helpful, kind, generous, or gentle. When correcting and redirecting a child's behavior, try not to say his name; save his name for the positive interactions.

Cross-merchandise. I noticed several years ago that maple syrup is generally on shelves with jams and jellies. In successful stores, syrup is also near the boxed pancake mix, as well as near the frozen waffles and French toast. Why? Someone with a carefully planned list will choose the syrup from the jam and jelly aisle. But another shopper may not consider syrup until after choosing a box of frozen Belgian waffles.

So it is in children's environments: A child who chooses the writing center expects to find paper and writing instruments there. The child building in the block area, though, may decide to put signs on a structure and then realize she needs paper and a pencil. If we follow retail's method of cross-merchandising, the child will have paper and pencils or markers in the block area, as well as in the writing center.

Design the space so customers will go all the way through it. Retailers know that many customers come in with one purpose in mind: Buy the dog food and go home. A well-designed retail interior will encourage that shopper to buy some milk, flowers, toothpaste, and a vase for the flowers, along with the dog food. They do this with attractive displays that call attention to the merchandise available in the store, and by making a variety of the same materials available at different spots within the store.

In children's classrooms, attractive displays can encourage children to try different areas of the room as well. We know that children's learning increases when they combine an assortment of simple materials in a variety of new ways because they are problem solving, inventing, and evaluating. How we display materials can entice them to try their hands at combining materials in new ways, too. And, if we make some of the same materials available throughout children's activity areas — books, for example, should be available in all areas, not just in the book corner — children will be motivated to put these books to use in their play in the block area, or in dramatic play.

Sudden changes in the environment confuse customers. Once, several years ago, I was in a popular retail store in the early morning. The grocery section of this store had been completely re-arranged, seemingly overnight. I saw an elderly gentleman who had stopped in the middle of an aisle and was simply leaning against his buggy. As I got closer to him, I heard his growling and complaining getting louder and more agitated. Finally, I heard him shout, "Where did they move the spaghetti? I can't find the spaghetti!"

Children who awaken from nap or come back to school after a weekend to find their classroom re-arranged can empathize with this man's frustration. It's difficult to play and engage deeply with mate-

rials in a classroom when those materials are no longer where a child expects them to be. We slow children down when we make them re-learn their learning environment. Does this mean children's environments are carved in stone? Absolutely not. Instead, rearrange and restructure environments based on children's needs and interests, but give them notice. Discuss the upcoming changes with them. Involve them. Let them participate in as much of the redesign as possible. Provide pictorial signs to guide them to new locations.

Label aisles so customers know where to find things. Although browsing in a new store can be pleasurable, any busy shopper will acknowledge frustration at not being able to find what they came for. People shop with specific goals in mind, and directional signs and labels help shoppers be successful. Shoppers don't have to wander around and waste time if a store's signage points them in the right direction.

In our classrooms, children can get right to work if the environment is well-organized and clearly labeled. Children become frustrated by messy and disorganized shelves. Labels should have both pictures and words, or real objects as well as pictures and words. When children can see what they need, they can get into their play quicker, and engage with materials for longer periods of time.

Minimize waiting. Recently, while I was waiting in line at the grocery store, the store manager walked up behind me and offered to open another line for me. Because I was in a line with my favorite cashier, I told him I was happy to wait in my line. In all other circumstances, I would have welcomed the additional cash register so I could quickly check out and go home.

In children's environments, we need to ensure that there are enough options, and enough duplicates of favorite materials, so that children don't have to wait excessively. Sometimes a child will prefer a particular toy or material and will be willing to wait even though other options are available. Let waiting be the child's choice when possible. When you see that children are consistently spending their time waiting for popular centers or equipment, provide duplicates, or open up additional areas for them.

Personalize. One size does not fit all. Retailers have learned that, although customers often share certain tastes and preferences, they are not all the same. Happy customers are those who have found stores that meet their individual needs. Successful retailers pay attention to shoppers' individual habits and preferences and make sure they can find the products they want. In classrooms, teachers should also pay attention to children's individual habits and preferences, and try to offer to them materials and experiences that meet these. Open-ended materials have no preconceived outcome or only one specific use: Think about providing sensory materials like sand and water, recyclable materials like cardboard boxes, plastic jar lids, cardboard tubes, lengths of fabric, and a variety of art media and writing instruments. When teachers provide materials that are more open-ended, children are more likely to choose them and combine them in ways that meet their own developmental needs.

Focus on customer service. What are the children telling you about their classroom? Retailers know that satisfied customers are more likely to return, and that customer feedback is necessary for them to continue to meet customers' needs. Focus groups are mainstays for researchers who poll a specific group or demographic for feedback. Early childhood programs need children's feedback, too. We won't know what to keep, change, move, and re-stock unless we take time to learn from those who use the space: children.

So, how do we survey children? Observation of their engagement levels and how they are using their activity areas give us a quick snapshot of their general satisfaction: A time sample over a 30-minute period, for example, will tell us which activity areas are getting the most usage (see time sample in Figure 1). Popular areas may need to be

re-stocked more often. Areas that are getting no use may need a complete overhaul. Form small focus groups of children and solicit input on what they want in these areas. If we want to know what children need in their environments, we need to ask.

Self-serve. Once while shopping with my daughter, I saw a blouse I liked and wanted to purchase. However, the color I wanted was hung high on a rack, far out of my reach. There was no associate nearby to assist me. I stretched, and jumped, and even looked for a ladder so that I could reach the blouse. Since I couldn't reach it, I didn't buy it. Successful retailers have their merchandise readily available and accessible to their customers so it can be purchased easily. Heavy items that require assistance are stored higher and bells are conveniently placed so customers can request assistance.

In children's classrooms, make materials and supplies readily available. Items that require adult assistance can be stored out of reach, but children need a system for requesting these items. Think about providing children with picture cards for these items

Figure 1

Time Sample
Observation – One-half (1/2) hour in five-minute increments

Area of Room:	9:00	9:05	9:10	9:15	9:20	9:25	9:30
Blocks	IIII	IIII	IIII	IIII	IIII	IIII	IIII
Art	II	∅	∅	I	I	∅	∅
Dramatic Play	IIII	IIII II	IIII I	IIII I	IIII	IIII	IIII
Writing Center	I	∅	∅	I	I	∅	∅
Science	∅	∅	∅	∅	∅	∅	∅
Manipulatives	II	III	III	II	III	III	III
Library	I	II	I	I	∅	I	II
Loft/ Climber (FBG Only)	II	II	I	I	II	II	I
Sensory Table	II	I	I	III	II	III	III
Watching/Moving Around	I	I	IIII	II	II	II	II

Summary Comments:

What's going on with the Art and Science areas? No one is playing in them! Check on supplies and re-stock if needed to make areas more engaging.

so that a child can choose a card and bring it to you when additional, or heavy, items are needed.

Minimize displays, but keep additional merchandise on hand. One of my students worked in retail for years. Her store was full of attractive displays, but with minimal stock on the shelves. Often, while shopping in her store, I would see an item I liked but would not see it in my size or favorite color. Each time, she went to their back storage area and found the item for me. The display space remained attractive and well-organized, allowing me to easily decide what I liked and wanted. Additional stock in a storage area allowed me to buy the exact item I wanted.

In children's classrooms, it's not feasible, nor desirable, that every material, prop, or supply be available to the children all the time. Too many materials on display can hinder a child's ability to choose. It is feasible, though, to keep extras of many items in nearby storage so that we can easily support children's play when additional materials are needed. Children's environments are learning places, and this learning occurs more naturally when children are happy, relaxed, and deeply engaged in their play. By applying what the retail world has already learned about how to create happy, relaxed, and engaging experiences for their customers, we can create stimulating and effective environments for young children.

Frances Carlson

Frances Carlson worked as a child care administrator for 20 years before beginning a career in higher ed. She currently teaches Early Childhood Education at Chattahoochee Technical College and at Mercer University's Tift College of Education. She is the author of two books, *Essential Touch* (2006) and *Big Body Play* (2011) and the DVD, *Expect Male Involvement* (2009). She has spoken nationally and internationally on these topics. She has three grown children, and a Norwegian Elkhound named Freya. In her free time, she rides her bike, goes to the beach, and cooks. You can contact her at: francescarlson@bellsouth.net

The Lifetime Value of a Loyal Customer

by Margaret Leitch Copeland and Susan Gimilaro

How are parents who are five minutes late treated in your center — as criminals or as valued lifetime customers?

Is a parent who is laid off treated as an automatic farewell or as an ongoing parent whose tuition is paid for through the hardship fund or bartered for other services?

Are parents whose children graduated from the program taken off the email list or recognized as permanent marketing champions receiving regular communications?

In *The Service Profit Chain*, Harvard Business School professors James Heskett, Earl Sasser, and Leonard Schlesinger (1997) offer two anecdotes — from Domino's Pizza and a Dallas Cadillac dealership — that illuminate the concept of valuing a lifetime customer. Experts estimate that the lifetime value of a loyal Domino's Pizza customer is $4,000 and a Dallas Cadillac customer is $332,000. In other words, far more than the day-to-day service or the individual pizza or car purchase. The authors note that these figures only represent the direct value of a lifetime customer and do not factor in the "value of referrals associated with satisfied customers" (p. 65).

Bartering Ideas*

- Ask staff to list the tasks that never get done.
- Add those to your list of unfinished tasks.
- Attach a value to each task.
- Be prepared before any parent gets laid off:
  — Painting indoors/outdoors
  — Writing grant proposals
  — Washing windows
  — Organizing parent groups
  — Creating/upgrading website
  — Laundering
  — Cleaning
  — Pruning trees
  — Making new curtains/pillowcases
  — Playground maintenance
  — Snow removal/raking roof
  — Cleaning closets
  — Organizing library materials
  — Cooking
  — Updating printed materials
  — Substituting (if qualified)

We know one center owner/director who bartered for a wedding planner!

*Check with your accountant to make sure taxes are paid on bartered services.

Responding to Valued Customers

Have you calculated the lifetime value of a loyal child care customer family in your program? Would parents be treated differently if they were thought of in terms of their lifetime value to the program? In the three scenarios above, programs that value life-time customers might offer the following responses:

To the parent who is late: "Oh, that's okay. We're all late sometimes! You can use one of the three 'Free Pass' cards you received for working on the play-ground project."

To the devastated parent who has been laid off: "We know this happens sometimes, which is why we established the fund where grandparents can make a donation and a local foundation contributes to help families who have come upon difficult times. We can help you for up to six weeks; after that, we would ask you to donate your time to defray the costs of your child(ren) staying in the program. We have a list of barter activities; we'll try to match your skills with our needs." (Be sure to mention the tax consequences of bartering.)

To parents whose children are aging out of your program: "Don't forget: We have a center reunion every June when families come back to see how their old friends are doing. It's so much fun now that we have been in business for 25 years. We have current parents who came here as infants them-selves! Be sure to send us any news you would like to have in the e-newsletter, and, of course, you can always advertise in it for free!"

Try calculating the lifetime value of a family in your program.

Sample: **Tuition for a family with 2 children**

Sample: **Referrals to their 2 neighbors**

■ Who then enroll one child each: .... + $141,292

■ Save on advertising: ....+ $500

---

78 weeks** @ infant rate of
$199/week x 2 children .... = $ 31,044

78 weeks @ toddler of
$186/week rate x 2 children .... = $ 29,016

156 weeks @ preschool rate
of $161 x 2 children .... = $ 50,232

100 weeks @ school-age rate
of $155 x 2 children .... = $ 31,000

Total .... = $ 141,292

*Based on New Hampshire 2007 Market Rate Survey of center-based programs

**78 weeks = 15 months; 156 weeks = 30 months; 100 weeks = 3 years of full-time and part-time after-school programming

In-kind services (Board participation, play-ground work days, pro bono legal work, donations of materials, collection of Box Tops for Education, website development, end of the year clean-up) .... + up to $50,000

Try calculating the cost of retaining the loyal customer who recruits new ones

■ Instead of the cost of Open Houses and advertis-ing, purchase tee-shirts for families that announce their 'brand loyalty' to your center: $1,000

■ Positive word-of-mouth advertising: $0

Of course the greatest value a family offers the center is their trust in the professionals who care for their treasured children!

What is the cost to the center to make the three scenarios in the introduction come true?

Cost of 'Free Pass' cards in late fees....................... $0

Lifetime Value Calculations for the _____ family

In-kind services from the family:

_____ $_____

_____ $_____

_____ $_____

_____ $_____

                    TOTAL $_____

Tuition Revenue:

___ weeks X $ ____ for infant care   X _____ child(ren) = $_____

___ weeks X $ ____ for toddler care X _____ child(ren) = $_____

___ weeks X $ ____ for preschool   X ____ child(ren) = $_____

___ weeks X $ ____ for school-age X _____ child(ren) = $_____

                    TOTAL $_____

Referrals:

_____ $_____

_____ $_____

_____ $_____

_____ $_____

                    TOTAL $_____

GRAND TOTAL = In-kind services + Tuition + Referrals $_____

Hint: Give the staff member who stays late a 'Free Pass' for the equivalent amount of time to offset his or her time and feelings.]

Cost of emailing newsletter to alumni families $0

Cost of annual potluck reunion............................. $0

Cost of safety net for laid-off parents*.................. $0

(*If funded by insurance fund or local foundation)

Net gain of bartering for service: Task gets done and lifetime customer is retained.

Compare these costs ($50 for t-shirts for the family) to the lifetime value of the customer ($283,084 + in-service value)!

Although at first it sounds very unlikely, there is a lot a child care business can learn from Domino's Pizza and a Cadillac dealer in Dallas! Directors of non-profit centers can ask parent board members to calculate their own lifetime values to make the point that a family's inability to pay full tuition for a period of time during the recession pales in comparison to a lifetime of loyalty and the provision of continuity of care for the family.

Reference

Haskett, J. L., Sasser, W. E., & Schlesinger, L. A. (1997). *The service profit chain*. New York: The Free Press

Margaret Leitch Copeland

Margaret Leitch Copeland, Ed.D., mentors and teaches leaders in early education and care. Visit www.leadershiplandscape.com.

Susan Gimilaro

Susan Gimilaro, M.A., is the Project Director for ACROSS NH where she works to provide professional development opportunities, consultation, and TA to after-school programs in New Hampshire. Susan has worked as a consultant, coach, and trainer in a variety of education settings, both locally and nationally. She has worked with early childhood programs, after-school programs, and public schools, as well as agencies and organizations that support quality initiatives in education. Her work focuses on adults working with youth. Whether in a public school, after-school program, or child care program, Susan helps adults bridge current research with their professional practice. She is passionate about bringing together a community of knowledgeable and skilled educators who can engage, support, and inspire learning in after-school staff and our youth.

Courting the Media with Special Events

by Karen Stephens

"Courting the media! Are you masochistic? The press views child care as a sure scoop on sexual abuse and sick kids. The farther away they stay from us the better." This statement reflects the views of many in child care. In the wake of considerable 'bad press' in the past, we have legitimate reasons for being gun-shy. Many feel as if we have been publicly vilified as a scapegoat for a variety of social ills and, therefore, shun relations with the media.

This article is going to challenge some of that defensiveness and urge you to work more with the media, not less. Here is an appeal to view the media objectively and to perceive it simply as a tool to be managed, not only for the benefit of children and families, but also for the child care profession.

Child care is on the vanguard of social change surrounding and involving the family. This can be threatening to a large percentage of the population who have never been in a child care setting as a child or have never used one for their own children. If we are to combat being the brunt of the public's suspicions and misconceptions, we have to become proactive rather than merely reactive. We must educate ourselves for utilizing the media in order to clearly communicate to the public who we are, what we do, and why.

Taking into consideration that 93% of adults in the United States listen to the radio regularly, 83% watch television, and 69% read newspapers (print and digital combined), it becomes apparent that the media can be a very effective and efficient tool for reaching the public. Through the media, we can reach the diverse coalition of people from whom we need support — namely the business sector, churches, funding agencies, elected officials, policy makers, and the voting public.

Now I know that you are already finding reasons for why you can't take the time for public relations via the media. With the garbage disposal backing up into the ventilation system, the furnace going on strike, and three teachers calling in sick, where do you find the time? Maybe you're afraid the media won't listen to you; after all, you're just a child care director. Perhaps you're fearful that they will make you talk into a camera (while the tape is rolling). Swallow your fears and do it anyway. Developing a positive image for child care and its workers is just too critical to be put on the back burner. Children deserve and desperately need informed, caring persons to speak on behalf of their best interests. Like it or not, one of those persons is you.

Promoting child care through purchased commercial advertising time is far beyond most of our means.

For a mere 30 seconds of advertising time, local television stations can charge from $700 to $900. National networks can command prices ranging from $50,000 to $100,000 depending on the time of day the commercial is aired. Obviously, child care must seek other methods for gaining access to the media.

Creating Media Events

Increasingly, child care providers are gaining access by creating media events that can be covered in news segments or talk shows of local and/or national programming. Many have had success in presenting child care as an exciting, effective family support service comprised of competent, caring professionals. Their efforts have been rewarded by increased name recognition and visibility, which helps in fundraising and recruitment. Their credibility has been enhanced as they encourage consumer awareness.

This article will identify the processes of creating successful media events. These include making an event newsworthy, selecting a skilled spokesperson, preparing for an interview, promoting the event, and following up on coverage.

Within the context of child care, a media event is a happening involving or relating to children and/or families. It is created with the intention of utilizing the media to help focus public attention on a particular topic, issue, or need. It can be large or small, but by design it is developed so that it will be perceived as newsworthy by the powers that be in media outlets. As the event is reported, a spokesperson will be asked for a statement or interview. When that time comes, it is up to the spokesperson to communicate how the event highlights the needs of children, families, and child care.

Meeting Mutual Needs

Before successfully breaking into the game of media monopoly, you have to be aware of the media's goals as well as your own. Be confident that you are meeting on equal ground. There is no reason to be intimidated. In reality, the media needs you just as much as you need them.

One of the goals of the media is to acquire reliable, credible, informed sources that can provide them with contemporary and relevant stories. They want this in order to appear sincerely concerned about the community. More importantly, they want stories that will build ratings. The higher the ratings, the more the media can charge advertisers for advertising time or space.

Thousands of families are in the throes of lifestyle changes that necessitate child care and support services. If the media is going to be responsive to those changes, they are going to have to use you as a source. Remember, you are the expert. You have the training and daily first-hand contact with families that make you uniquely qualified to contribute to public discussion.

Making an Event Newsworthy

How do you package an event in order to spark the media's attention? It is a matter of providing them with an *angle*. They need some justification for presenting the event to their audience. The following examples dramatize the underlying principles.

Make a visual statement. During the *Week of the Young Child*, four centers of Illinois State University, Bloomington-Normal, Illinois, paraded balloon and sign-carrying children onto a campus quadrangle, each coming from the north, south, east, or west. They met in the center for a group singalong and *pep rally*. The event was designed to show that child care from all areas was coming together in a united effort for a common cause.

Make it action packed and colorful. The launching of a hot air balloon at the Washington Monument with hundreds of children's smiling faces was an event created by Children's World in Washington, DC, to celebrate the *Week of the Young Child*. The event provided pizzazz to what might have first appeared as just another national week.

The 4 C's of Central Florida, Inc. cosponsors a Children's Festival each year around Lake Eola in Orlando, Florida. Over 150 human service organizations set up activity booths for children and pass out printed material on their programs to parents. The festival represents a vast coalition and boasts of 8,000 visitors each year. The media's interest is further peaked by Disney World characters parading about and NASA astronauts mingling with the crowd. Throw in some music, clowns, a train, and pony rides, and you can't keep the press away.

The Massachusetts Association of Day Care Agencies sponsored a Look Up to Day Care Day. Held in Boston Commons (you remember, the setting for *Make Way for Ducklings*), children and child care workers simultaneously released hundreds of helium-filled balloons into the heavens. Music and face painting were the finishing touches to attract the media.

Karen Miller, national education director for Children's World, appeared on a television talk show featuring creativity and imagination. With imagination of her own, she was able to turn the studio audience into the event. Illustrating that sensory experiences help to trigger creativity in children, she distributed gallons of homemade silly putty to the entire audience. The cameras couldn't pull away from the expressions of adults who were for the first time experiencing the squishy, slimy joys of silly putty! The phone lines rang off the hook with home viewers requesting the recipe!

Highlight local responses to national issues or trends. At a time when the arms race was in the news daily, and capitalizing on the national notoriety of Dr. Seuss's *Butter Battle Book*, I was able to persuade a television station to tape six children, ages 10 to 14, while they discussed the issues raised in the book and related them to current events. As a result of that coverage, a radio station interviewed me regarding children's perceptions of the arms race.

Many centers have taken advantage of the media's interest in child sexual abuse by presenting prevention programs on the topic for children and parents. The media has interviewed child care staff and parents and taped children as they participated.

Peg Delaney and Julie Cassady, student teachers from the Illinois State University Home Economics Department, created an aerobics program for children. Parents and children, in leg warmers and sweatbands, participated with plenty of jump and jive. The media related the story to the national fitness craze.

Involve a public official. The 4 C's of Central Florida, Inc. hosts an annual child care tour. An event that started 13 years ago in an old, beat up, non-air-conditioned school bus has now become a luxury event in a plush chartered bus. The tour takes key officials, decision makers, and the press to where the action is — child care operating in full swing. The tour guide takes advantage of the captive audience during transport and explains child care funding, program diversity, licensing regulations, and the needs of child care.

Elinor Guggenheimer, then president of the Child Care Action Campaign, relates the story of a center that invited public officials to visit and relive life as three-year-olds. The press relished reporting the traffic jam antics of the mayor and police commissioner as they explored the block area.

Groups of people make news. Conferences often gain attention because of the sheer numbers of people involved. When hosting the Midwest AEYC annual conference, Minnesota AEYC brought their theme, "Follow the Rainbow," to life by literally painting a rainbow on the two blocks of sidewalk that connected the two conference hotels. Via the media, the whole city watched as it was created with none other than the city mayor in the lead.

Focus on the unique. Pat Clark, director of Westmorland Children's Center in Bethesda, Maryland, was requested to provide babysitting at the hotel site for the Annual Arab Anti-Discrimination Committee Conference. Focusing on their stated commitment to human rights, Pat was able to convince the group to take a stand for quality child care and good working conditions for caregivers as basic human rights. Two hotel suites were transformed into a child care center. Children enjoyed quality care — appropriate group size and low ratios. Caregivers were paid well and worked six-hour shifts. Reporters from Africa, Japan, France, Germany, and the United States were attracted to the unique situation and the statement that it was making.

Realizing that most people have not been inside a child care center, Marlene Stoiber, director of Early Childhood Services for Neighborhood Centers, Inc., took a sample to the people. Her organization set up a typical classroom in a shopping mall. The classroom was fully equipped and featured self-selected activities. The *center* enrolled children for half an hour at a time.

Announce a new service. Mary Lee Johns, director of Children and Youth Services for the Texas Conference of Churches, reports that a parents' *Warmline* received positive attention. The project is a hotline for parents who are on the verge of abusing their child. *Warmline* also sponsored "Parent Tip of the Week" on local radio stations.

The McLean County AEYC caught the attention of the public by combining efforts with a crisis line to provide *PhoneFriend*, a hotline for latchkey children. McLean County AEYC also made the news when it coordinated efforts with a radio station and police department to provide free fingerprinting of children. Information on preventing child abduction was also distributed.

Make it timely. Patty Siegel, executive director of the California Child Resource and Referral Network, and Merle Lawrence, research director for the same organization, created the *Child Care Information Kit*, which created quite a stir in the media. The kit itself is designed to educate policy makers, employers, and the media on the needs, supply, and policy issues surrounding child care in the San Francisco Bay area.

Its exposure and acceptance was maximized by timing its distribution with a press conference announcing that the White House Office on Private Sector Initiatives had come to town. The White House's envoy had come to convince Bay Area executives to become involved in child care for their employees. The kit was just the tool needed by employers and the media as they were trying to understand the nature of child care problems faced by parents. The kit was released in March 1984 and is still receiving attention from the press, most recently Patty Siegel's appearance on CBS's national morning news.

Selecting a Spokesperson

Before you contact the media about your event, select an official spokesperson. This person serves as a liaison with the media. It may be the director, a teacher, or board member of your program. Because this person will greatly affect your public image, she should be personable, enthusiastic, articulate, and well informed about your program.

The role of the spokesperson is to develop a positive working relationship with members of the media so that they will be receptive to story ideas. Assigning one person to communicate with the public also projects an organized image. Reporters won't cover an event if they have to track down three or four people in order to get the complete story.

One of the major challenges for the spokesperson is to become adept at the art of being interviewed.

Preparing for Interviews

An interview provides you with your real chance to communicate with the public. Before embarking on this adventure, it's important to develop some savvy in regards to the interview process.

Identify your goals. What do you want to communicate? Speaking from experience, Pat Clark believes, "If you know what you want to say, you have at least half a chance at getting your message across in an undistorted manner."

A positive attitude is invaluable. "Style and flamboyance gets the media's attention," according to Phoebe Carpenter, executive vice president of 4 C's of Central Florida, Inc. Karen Miller calls it "enthusiasm that shows you have a life commitment to the cause."

Be well prepared. Sandra Mathers, reporter for the *Orlando Sentinel* in Florida, says that a reporter needs an interviewee who has her facts and figures together. By being organized and concise, you help to make the reporter's job easier, and that always wins a few points. Present your statements in a clear, logical manner. Feel free to let the interviewer know the types of questions about child care that you usually encounter. Some programs develop a media kit that concisely describes their program through a brochure, fact sheets, and position statements.

Keep your message short and sweet. If you ramble on, your point is likely to be missed. A print reporter may be able to take the time to sift through your comments; but in a television interview, you may have only 20 to 60 seconds to respond.

Anticipate key questions and your response. Be aware of what the hot topics in current events are so that you may respond in an intelligent manner. Your response may involve giving facts, figures, anecdotes, or opinions.

Tie in real life examples. Mathers states that the media likes to dramatize issues with actual examples of persons involved. Patty Siegel fills this need by presenting the media with *consumer profiles* — examples of parents grappling with the issues of availability, affordability, and quality.

State your ideas in a positive way. Say "Child care can help to establish good health habits in young children," rather than "I know most people think that day care kids are sick because we don't make them wash their hands, but that just isn't so."

Relax and act natural. You want to appear as if you are enjoying the interview. If you appear tense, it will color the image that you project.

Practice for television interviews. Dress professionally and look neat. A jacket looks professional and provides a lapel for clipping a microphone. Avoid white clothing and flashy jewelry; they both reflect too much light, which produces a glare and poor picture. Look at the reporter when you speak, not into the camera and not downward.

Beth Fredericks, director of Children's Village in Cambridge, Massachusetts, advises interviewees to be flexible and accommodating when dealing with reporters, their cords, lights, and semi-egotistical hurried attitudes. The temporary inconvenience to you and your program should be offset by the greater good of receiving positive media exposure.

Promoting the Event

You've decided on the event, chosen a spokesperson, and are prepared for the interview. It is now a matter of promoting the event to the media. You have to identify your media sources so you can let them know who you are and what you are doing.

Compiling a media list. Most Chamber of Commerce offices maintain a list of local media, which identifies their name, type of medium (print, radio, television), address, and phone number. This list can usually be purchased for a small fee.

Many lists also identify the designated gatekeepers. These are media contact people who have the power to assign and often edit stories. They ultimately decide what gets into the news and in what form. These are the people to whom you direct your request for coverage. Their titles vary; but they are typically called news director, assignment editor, producer, or other official sounding title. To this list add deadline dates for press releases and story ideas. If you plan an event too close to a deadline, you may not receive coverage. To the list you should also add in-house newsletters of companies and organization newsletters of major employers in your area. They are another means for reaching the public. If your Chamber of Commerce does not provide a media list, you may need to call each media organization directly to track down the needed information.

Analyzing your media sources. After identifying your media, analyze their publications or broadcasts. What type of stories do they run and who covers them? What type of talk shows do they air? Which columnists do they feature? What is their political leaning and the tone of their editorials? What sections of their publications would be interested in child care articles. In these times, the answer may include the financial section as well as family living and education. The answers to these questions will influence how you organize your event and present it to each media source.

Sending press releases. Press releases are used to alert the media to your event. There are many guides available to show you how to make one. You can also ask for a sample of the preferred format for each media source.

In general, you should answer the questions what, who, where, when, and why. Put it all in the first paragraph if possible. The media is busy and swamped with requests for coverage; if your first paragraph doesn't grab them, into the wastebasket it goes.

Type the release (double spaced) and put the name, address, and phone number of your organization in the top left-hand corner. Under that, put your spokesperson's name and phone number for further questions. In the top right-hand corner, type the release date for the information (i.e., For Immediate Release or For Release on April 12, 2016).

It is extremely important to hand deliver your release, at least when you are beginning to establish

a relationship. It provides you with the opportunity to talk personally with reporters and gatekeepers. The rapport that you establish will be invaluable in requesting coverage.

Public service announcements. Public service announcements (PSAs) are used to inform the public about an event; they also help to remind the media that you are around. Contact your media for specific information on how to submit them and in what form. Many media outlets have a community affairs director or someone similar. If you are a non-profit agency, they may help you to write and produce PSAs.

Personal contacts with the media. Patty Siegel warns child care providers not to wait for the media to come to them. "You have to cultivate the media by going to them and keeping in touch." Keeping in touch may include phone calls, sending them your newsletter, or dropping a note of congratulations on a good story (even if you weren't mentioned). Some centers are trying to recruit media representatives to serve on their advisory boards.

Remember one thing about reporters: they always want to appear objective and unbiased. When approaching them for coverage, it is best if they perceive that you are promoting child care in general and not just your own personal gain. Reporters are very wary of self-interest. It is wises to promote yourself and organization as one among many who are trying to improve the quality of services provided to children and families.

Following Up on Coverage

After conducting an event, it is important to evaluate the level of success you experienced in courting the media. You should assign at least one person to review your coverage (or lack of it) in each media source. Note the strengths and weaknesses of the story. Did you get your message across? What quotes or examples were highlighted? What did the media play up most? The answers will help you in planning

---

What Not to Do:

- Don't ask why a feature, story, or photo isn't used.

- Never send a release without some type of release date on it, where the editor can see it clearly and immediately.

- Don't overuse the name of your organization in the copy. Don't use all capital letters for your business name or the name of your project.

- Don't call up editors or news directors asking if material is going to be used or asking for clippings or air times.

---

your next event. Save any print coverage for future reference.

Sending thank-yous. Remember that everyone needs strokes. You are likely to enjoy the spotlight of the media again if you reinforce their efforts. One way to stroke is to make phone calls and send letters. The letters should express your respect and appreciation for the time and effort expended by the reporter. Letters should go directly to the reporter who covered the event with copies being sent to her superiors (i.e., news director, managing editor, general manager). Writing a *Letter to the Editor* column shows that you felt the community was well served.

About misrepresentation. In the words of Phoebe Carpenter, "If you want the benefit of publicity, you have to be willing to take the risk of being misquoted." If you find that you have been misquoted or misrepresented, it is probably best to ignore it and chalk it up to experience. For future reference, determine how you could have restructured or rephrased a comment in order to project your views more clearly. Problems with inaccuracy can be the result of giving too much information in technical language in a disorganized fashion.

If you feel that a slanted view against you was blatant and intentional, you can talk to the reporter or editor in a cooperative manner. Remember, you want to salvage the relationship so you have a second and third shot of presenting your views accurately.

If you are still not satisfied, you can write a *Letter to the Editor*, and that's about it. You'll just have to pick up the pieces and go on from there.

In Ending

Positive media coverage for child care and related services can be attained. It takes goal setting, planning, imagination, and a lot of persistent work. Fluke publicity may put us in the limelight from time to time, but an ongoing public relations campaign is required if we are to increase the image of child care. Through our combined efforts, we can make an impact on the way that we are perceived and supported.

Karen Stephens

Karen Stephens, M.S. in education specializing in early childhood, began her career as a teacher in a preschool classroom in 1975. From 1980 to May 2013 she served as campus child care director and taught child development and early childhood program administration courses for the Illinois State University's Department of Family and Consumer Sciences. Today she writes from her home and enjoys occasional travel to deliver staff development training and conference presentations.

Dancing with an Octopus

The Graceful Art of Collaboration

by Elizabeth Morgan Russell

Have you just had a great idea that would make your community a better place to live for children and families, and you know you can't accomplish your goal alone? Or, perhaps, after talking with other child care professionals, you've identified a common need or interest and a small group of colleagues actually wants to do something about your shared concern.

Collaboration — working with like-minded others to achieve a common purpose — is an action-oriented strategy (Carter, 2003) that you might want to consider as a way of reaching your goals. Because collaboration, as in dancing with an octopus (Dunkle & Nash, 1989), requires keeping track of many different points (or tentacles), planners who know when collaborations are more likely to work and what potential missteps could occur, are more likely to move with grace and style toward their goal(s). After reading this article, you will be able to list at least three:

■ characteristics of successful collaborative projects.

■ potential missteps and strategies for avoiding, lessening, or resolving barriers to successful collaborative activities.

■ examples of collaborative activities for parents or providers.

Why Dance?

Generally, individuals, agencies, or organizations collaborate because they believe that together they can accomplish what could not be done alone. Also, their participation in the collaboration enables organizations and agencies to reach their program objectives (Bergman, 2003). In the field of early education and care, collaborations are frequently formed in order to improve services, and/or the systems that deliver the services, by:

■ increasing the quality and quantity of services for children and families.

■ ensuring more equitable distribution of services.

■ minimizing expenses and service duplication.

■ addressing staff and space shortages.

■ equalizing regulations across early childhood programs (i.e., ensuring high-quality standards are required for all forms of child care).

■ improving training opportunities.

■ building public support and advocacy for early care and education (Kagan & Rivera, p. 52, 1991).

You may want to pause and consider within which of the above seven areas your collaborative idea falls. Can you think of other reasons for collaborating in the field of early education and care?

Collaborations may be short- or long-term; have local, state, or national memberships; focus on one or multiple goals; and include three or more partners. One agency may participate in more than one collaborative project.

Pause for a moment and consider the following questions: What are some of the collaborative projects that you have heard about or participated in? Do you think they were successful? Chances are, if the collaborations were successful, they shared certain characteristics. The following section provides an overview of some of the characteristics of successful collaborations.

How Do You Keep the Octopus from Stepping on Your Toes?

An anagram of 'octopus' will provide the framework for a discussion about the characteristics of successful collaborations and potential missteps:

> **O** rganization
> **C** limate
> **T** eam
> **O** wnership
> **P** rogress
> **U** nderstanding
> **S** hare

Organization: One or more members of the collaboration, perhaps you, must take the lead role in organizing the planning efforts of the larger group. This core group of individuals (or planning group) recruits additional members for the collaboration, calls the meetings, sets the initial agenda, chairs the meetings, keeps the group on track and focused, takes and distributes minutes, keeps all the members of the collaboration informed of the group's activities and progress, and ensures that all members have an opportunity to be heard and to make tangible contributions to the collaboration's success (Malloy, Rodriguez, & Chance, 1996). Once the collaboration is underway, the membership of the core planning group can change in order to share the leadership responsibilities and avoid burnout.

Climate: A climate of cooperation or one of competition between collaboration members will have a profound influence upon the success or failure of the group's activities. If members have competed or are competing for the same service delivery area, clients (e.g. parents, children), funding or other resources, this must be acknowledged and resolved (Morgan & Spearly, 1983). In order for the collaboration to be successful, the members must agree that the shared goal takes precedence over issues of turf-ism (Shaw, 2003). Members who have previously participated in successful collaborations can be asked how their group resolved issues of competition and turf-ism. Time, open discussions, and a shared focus can frequently, although not always, build a climate of cooperation, and a feeling among the collaboration's members that they are all part of the same team.

Team: Successful collaborative teams demonstrate these characteristics (Malloy, Rodriguez, Chance, & Reid, 1997):

■ Members, or at least a core group of the membership, regularly attend meetings.

■ The membership is diverse and representative of any group that has a stake in the outcome of the collaboration.

■ Meetings are held on a regular basis to maintain group momentum.

■ Conflict resolution strategies used by group members strengthen rather than divide the team.

■ Consensus is used to make decisions: "Although I may not be in 100% agreement, I can live with and support this decision."

■ Members share responsibilities for achieving the collaboration's goal.

- The goal is in written form and was developed through consensus.

- The work plan and timeline are written and referred to on a regular basis.

- All members feel a strong sense of ownership in the collaboration.

- Periodic comparison of your collaboration's dynamics to the list could prove to be a useful self-evaluation exercise.

Ownership: Without a sense of ownership or 'buy-in' from group members, the collaboration is doomed from the start: attendance at meetings will decline, timelines will not be met, tasks will be done incompletely or not at all. It is essential that members of the collaboration feel emotionally and professionally responsible for the success of the project. The core group of planners can help members to buy-in by using initial meeting(s) to reach consensus on these issues:

- Why are we here? What needs to be done?

- What will this collaboration look like?

- What are the benefits of participation in the collaboration for my clients, co-workers, staff, and/or agency?

- Who is missing? Who else do we need to invite?

- What are the ground rules for resolving conflict, decision-making (e.g. consensus, majority vote), respecting diverse opinions and perspectives of collaboration members, turn-taking during meetings, wandering from the topic during meetings, poor attendance at meetings, setting agendas for meetings, determining meeting frequency, date and times, and communicating with each other between meetings?

- Who is responsible for doing what?

Although some members may feel impatient or frustrated with the time spent building ownership, these initial steps are the basis of the complicated dance of collaboration. Time, hurt feelings, and the success of the project can be the costs of moving forward without buy-in.

Progress: Once an initial sense of ownership has been established, ongoing enthusiasm and investment in the collaboration can be fostered through regular progress reports. Members need to know their work is going somewhere (Malloy, Rodriguez, & Chance, 1996; 1997). Everyone is busy; dance cards are full. Periodic, brief progress reports, which center around key questions — Where have we been? Where are we going? How far do we have to go? Do we need to change directions? — will help members assess the progress of the project and determine when adjustments to the work plan and timeline are needed. "The members of successful collaborations understand that a change of direction is not negative, but natural, and — if used well — is an opportunity for growth" (Kagan & Rivera, p. 54, 1991).

Understanding: An understanding of what resources (e.g. time, energy, expertise, contacts, funding, meeting space, supplies, postage, and so on) each member will commit to the collaboration should be established during the initial meetings of the project. In addition to building ownership, itemizing resources will help members determine if any resources necessary to the success of the collaboration are inadequate or missing. Some or all members of the collaboration must take responsibility for gathering the missing resources.

Share: Shared leadership, decision-making power (Shaw, 2003), ownership, and resources are characteristics of successful collaborations. In addition to being a basic step in the collaborative dance, shared leadership is an avenue for professional development. Early education and care professionals who have experience in leadership roles have the opportunity to expand their repertoire of group management strategies by watching other leaders in action. Simultaneously, novice leaders are exposed to a variety of styles and can practice their skills in a safe setting through the mentorship of their more experienced peers. Some participants in the collaboration, particularly members of the initial planning group, may have difficulty letting go of their leadership role. Group members may have difficulty in relinquishing their leadership role because they are so invested in the project and have thought so long about it, that they have formed a mental picture of what the collaboration 'should look like.' Remembering the shared goal of the project and accepting the fact that input from others will alter the final picture may help these members modify their expectations. Setting up a system for sharing leadership early on in the collaboration could make it easier for members to rotate and share this responsibility.

Because it takes a group of dedicated individuals to make a collaboration work, it is important to share credit for the success of the project with all members. Gratitude can be shown between members throughout the collaboration with letters, tokens (e.g. personalized mugs), food (e.g. 'Thank-You cakes'), cards, or fun awards (e.g. 'Trial-by-fire' certificate). Members of the project must be nurtured so they are better able to nurture the collaboration. Public acknowledgements of project success should recognize all members; each member's contribution to the success of the project is unique and essential.

Sharing the process as well as the outcome of collaborations with colleagues in the early education and care profession extends the benefits of the members' work to their communities, children, and families.

So You Just Want to Dance

In summary, an unsuccessful collaboration is like an octopus out of water; it flails clumsily around and goes nowhere. Alternatively, when all members of the collaboration are moving in the same direction, that is, when the collaboration includes a core planning group, fosters cooperation and teamwork, builds ownership for the project, encourages pooling of resources, and distributes leadership and decision-making power among members, phenomenal distance toward the goal can be covered through a powerful, efficient and, at times, graceful group effort.

For Additional Information

Bergman, R. (2000). Building collaborations between programs and within the community. *Exchange, 124,* 55-57.

Carter, M. (2003). Walking the talk of collaboration. *Exchange, 150,* 72-74.

Dunkle, M., & Nash, M., (1989). Creating effective interagency collaboratives. *Education Week, 8*(25), p. 44.

Kagan, S. L., & Rivera, A. M. (1991). Collaboration in early care and education: What can and should we expect? *Young Children, 47*(1), 51-56.

Malloy, P., Rodriguez, C. R., & Chance, G. (1996). *The tool kit: A collection of activities to support collaboration and early care and education.* Austin, TX: Head Start State Collaboration Office.

Malloy, P., Rodriguez, C. R., Chance, G., & Reid, C. W. (1997). *A workbook guide to developing a local career development plan.* Austin, TX: Head Start State Collaboration Office.

Morgan, E. L., & Spearly, D. H. (1983). *Child care consortiums by employers: Four interorganizational issues to consider when developing a joint project.* Austin, TX: Austin Child Guidance Center.

Shaw, M. M. (2003). Successful collaboration between the nonprofit and public sectors. *Nonprofit Management & Leadership, 14*(1), 107-120.

Elizabeth Morgan Russell

Elizabeth Morgan Russell possesses expertise in policy-directed research and analysis, organization management, training and curriculum development, writing and editing, and educational event planning. Dr. Morgan Russell also brings relevant family policy connections and a recognized and awarding-winning commitment to children and families.

Building Strong Bonds with Program Sponsors

by Karen Stephens

Some directors in the child care field are autonomous. We own and operate our own programs. Such *stand-alone* program directors are beholden to family clients, licensing, and perhaps accreditation agencies, but not to a higher layer of bureaucracy. However, the majority of child care programs collaborate with other groups to provide services. We depend upon an assortment of program sponsors and/or funding agencies. For instance, some of us are housed in religious institutions, parks and recreation programs, universities, corporations, community social service agencies, high schools, malls, or even grocery stores.

When a child care center is housed within a larger organization, our programs function as a small cog in a much larger wheel. Such centers are subject to decisions umbrella organizations make in terms of facilities, utility payments, custodial services, and a host of other issues that crop up unexpectedly. If implications for child care are not considered throughout the decision making process, the quality of child care operation can be jeopardized.

Programs that are dependent on the support of larger sponsors have unique challenges. Surviving and thriving depends on the depth of good will directors can muster from sponsors and funders. For stability and continuity of services, a wise child care director consistently works to build and maintain strong financial as well as emotional bonds with upper-level administration or bureaucracy.

First, second, and last, child care is a people business. The bottom-line to building bonds with sponsors and funding personnel is striking up relationships. Those relationships must be nurtured with time and effort. Only then can trusting, respectful, and appreciative partnerships develop and deepen. We need to cultivate those relationships across supervisory lines and throughout all sponsor departments or divisions.

Child care directors are used to considering the needs, wants, and desires of teaching and caregiving staff. And we're good at anticipating positive ways to respond to children and families. But we're not always as good at responding to those who touch children's lives from beyond our child care doors. To receive the support we need, it's essential to make other groups feel good about helping our child care programs.

Directors aren't the only child care staff who play a role in public relations. True partnerships include all child care staff. Whenever possible, spread sponsor relationship duties around. It's a great way to develop and mentor staff onto new skills. And it builds sponsor respect for the entire child care operation.

This article will supply you with plenty of proven public relations strategies. Some listed will be simple, short-term, and inexpensive. Others will be complex, ongoing, and require a budget line item. All can be customized to your individual situation. If you put even a few into practice, you'll create a stronger support system for your center. And you'll remind sponsors and funders they can play an important role in helping children. That's a good thing to do in life; child care staff shouldn't have a monopoly on it.

Starting Out

Identify Your Public Relations Message

Before you select a public relations activity, identify your goal. What do you want to achieve? What message do you want to communicate? What do you want sponsors and funders to believe about their involvement in your program?

Once you identify your message, fine-tune it. Write down the core message(s) you want to consistently communicate to center allies. When you know what you hope to achieve, you are better able to create suitable public relations strategies. Listed are some samples of messages you may want to communicate:

- Your center exists as an important, useful unit within the sponsor's organization.

- Sponsors are a vital partner in achieving your center's goals and mission.

- Sponsors impact your program operation whenever they make decisions.

- Sponsors can take pride in the services they support, which help families.

- Sponsors are part of a caring community that helps ensure your center's welfare.

- Sponsors have a right to reap rewards and share in the joy of knowing children.

- Sponsors are helping children when they are most responsive to nurturing.

- Sponsors make a positive impact on families by supporting high-quality child care operations.

- Sponsors invest in the community and the future by helping children and families today.

Public Relations Strategies

Don't Let Them Forget Your Center Exists

- Send sponsors well-written monthly newsletters with attractive graphics.

- Make sure they see your name. Use good signage on your play yard, classrooms, and vans.

- Remind sponsors of your website and keep it updated regularly.

- Occasionally (but not too often) email sponsor representatives with good news about your program.

- When sending reports to sponsors, include a photo of your child care kids they can post on their bulletin board.

- Have center t-shirts for children to wear on field trips and walks.

- Ask sponsors to add your child care website as a link on their website.

- Where there is shared space, such as display windows or bulletin boards in foyers, ask volunteers to set up engaging, attractive displays that reflect your program's activities.

- Ask if you can post matted and framed children's art in the sponsor's hallways. Be SURE to label it prominently with your center's name and the artist's first name and age.

- Provide business cards for all child care staff so sponsors get to know more than just the director.

- In your entryway, have good photos posted of all staff with a brief biography.

Make Them Part of the Child Care Family

■ Each setting has its own administrative structure and jargon; learn it. Show respect by knowing names and titles of those in the organizational chart. Address sponsors accordingly until they ask you to be less formal.

■ Invite sponsors in for celebrations or special events; introduce them around.

■ Include sponsors meaningfully in activities. For instance, a grand opening of a children's hair salon in the dramatic play corner requires a ribbon cutting ceremony. Ask a program sponsor to do the honors.

■ Ask sponsor representatives to share their unique talents in a classroom.

■ Include sponsors on appropriate, engaging field trips.

■ Make a 'Family Tree' of the child care center. At the base, include sponsors; of course, ask for real photos to include.

■ When holding dedications for a new addition or play yard, ask sponsors to speak or introduce a special honoree.

■ If your program or program staff are featured in local media, do your best to get the reporter to include your sponsor's name in some way. Sponsors like to be recognized for their efforts.

■ Remember sponsor's staff during holidays. For instance, children can make goodie bags to give to the cooks in the food service staff.

■ Ask sponsors to be on your child care advisory committee.

■ Ask sponsor representatives to be guest readers for a story time. (Give them tips for succeeding, so their experience is fun!)

■ On Secretary's or Boss's day, have the children deliver a bouquet of flowers or cookies to sponsors.

Become a Part of the Sponsor's Family

■ Attend special functions a sponsor holds, such as year-end awards or annual reports or campus quad festivities.

■ Serve on planning committees and contribute to the function in some way. For instance, children can make centerpieces or artwork for a luncheon. A child care staff member can take a speaker to lunch or pick them up from the airport.

■ Serve on committees that are important to the organization, such as a parking committee.

■ Offer to contribute a small article for their newsletter or website.

■ Ask to be included on facility tours that sponsors give to visitors, including business, government, philanthropic, or international partnership tours.

■ Volunteer to present a program for the sponsor's Wellness Program. Topics that offer tips for managing work and family are very popular.

■ Enhance your shared environment. A friend from a church-sponsored program enhanced the area just outside her classrooms with a pew filled with pillows, plants, framed photos of program staff, and an aquarium. It became a popular spot among the whole church congregation, especially the elderly who liked to watch the fish and "listen to the sweet sounds of children."

■ Serve on community committees on behalf of your sponsor. For instance, volunteer to work at a county fair or a career fair for the sponsor.

■ Depending on your sponsor relationship, offer to put up rotating displays in boardrooms, reception areas, or student unions.

■ If the sponsor has an in-house newsletter, submit details about your staff's achievements or conference attendance to be included. It builds your center's credibility as well as your sponsor's respect for staff qualifications.

- During anniversary or founders day celebrations, find ways to include the child care children. For instance, if your company is 50 years old, children can present a 50th birthday cake at a function. (However, don't have the kids blow out the candles. It's tempting, but… not sanitary.)

- Ask to be an agenda speaker for orientation of new sponsor staff. Some college programs provide evening child care for new faculty/staff who attend new employee meetings. Others provide child care during key events, such as a weekend theatrical play or sports activity.

- Ask that your program be given a little space in the sponsor's public brochure. One director was able to get information about her child care center in her school's basketball programs that were given to all spectators.

- If a sponsor's statewide, regional, or national leadership meet in your locale, offer to give a brief presentation. Be prepared with key facts you can cite off the top of your head.

Give Public Thanks and Recognition When It's Due

- Hold recognition functions with families served present. Encourage them to thank the sponsors.

- Nominate key sponsor representatives for community awards. Most communities have service, education, or business awards that are advertised in the media.

- Write *Letters to the Editor* of your local media to praise your sponsor's support or a specific good deed or improvement the sponsors made possible.

- Present plaques or certificates for outstanding support. Frame them so they are sure to be posted on a sponsor's wall.

- Send written memos to sponsors when their employees do a good job for the child care program. For instance, a good custodian deserves to get a letter of thanks sent to his boss. In the letter, ask that it be considered during the custodian's evaluation time. For efforts above and beyond the call of duty, send complimentary letters up through the whole chain of command to a CEO or president. All the supervisors in between get some of the credit then, too.

Pass Along Some Childhood Fun

- Have a small group of cheerful children unexpectedly deliver *certificates of appreciation* to sponsor offices.

- Invite sponsors to view fun classroom festivities, such as pumpkin painting.

- Anytime of year go caroling down sponsor hallways with the kids.

- When you send out memos, include a snack-size bag of candy, colorful stickers, or a teeny bottle of blowing bubbles. The surprise is a great way to reconnect sponsors to their own fond childhood memories.

- When an ally of the center has a birthday, as a surprise have children sing "Happy Birthday" on their voice mail.

- Name a child care feature after a sponsoring organization. For instance, you could name a butterfly garden for the United Way staff or a play yard gazebo for the Urban League.

- Hold well-organized book fairs or toy fairs on a sponsor's site so their staff can conveniently buy holiday gifts for children in their lives.

- When your program families attend an evening or weekend children's concert together, invite program sponsors and their families, too.

Share Your Successful Ideas!

If you have more proven public relations ideas, please pass them along to me. You can find me at our child care's website: www.childcarecenter.ilstu.edu. Best of luck getting the sponsor support your center deserves.

Karen Stephens

Karen Stephens, M.S. in education specializing in early childhood, began her career as a teacher in a preschool classroom in 1975. From 1980 to May 2013 she served as campus child care director and taught child development and early childhood program administration courses for the Illinois State University's Department of Family and Consumer Sciences. Today she writes from her home and enjoys occasional travel to deliver staff development training and conference presentations.

Making Your Website an Effective Marketing Partner

by Julie Wassom

The Internet has become a primary way your enrollment prospects move from information gathering to readiness to buy. While most parents will make their final child care decision only after the face-to-face contact that comes during a center visit, an increasing number of inquiry source reports cite the Internet as the place early education prospects go to investigate centers worth visiting. This makes the Internet an important part of the purchasing process.

Is it important for your early care and education business to have a presence on the Internet? Absolutely! Having a good website is an essential marketing tool for attracting today's buyers of your child care services. Without it, some prospects will not even know you exist. As you design or refine your website, you will get a greater return on your investment if you make it more than an online brochure that merely educates visitors about your center and your services. It must also be a marketing tool that helps you generate inquiries, secure center visits, convert the visits into enrollments, and serve your customers and other referral sources.

■ What will make your website a more effective inquiry generator?

■ How can you build your site so search engines (and your ideal customer) will find you?

■ What are the best techniques for driving qualified prospects to your website?

For answers to these and other questions about website marketing, I interviewed two Internet marketing experts: Anita Larson and Heather Lutze. Anita is an Internet marketing speaker, author, and consultant who fuses common sense with technology and believes in the powerful, global effect of a great website. Her company, The Web Muse, helps businesses attract ideal clients to their websites. Heather is the owner of Findability Group, a firm offering boutique search marketing services, including Pay Per Click (PPC), Search Engine Optimization (SEO), and social media. Heather, a recognized authority on search engine marketing strategies, is author of *The Findability Formula* (John Wiley & Sons, 2009). Anita's and Heather's responses confirmed many of my own recommendations for effective website marketing and added several more tips.

Julie: Why should every early care and education program have a website?

Anita: Because more and more people are using the Internet to search and the Internet constitutes a large percentage of their search. Many people want to see something visual before making contact, and a good website can give them that.

Julie: When a child care business owner is designing a website, what are some key considerations that will cause the site to more effectively help them market the center and its services?

Anita: First, determine who you are trying to reach. What is the goal of the site? What do you want to have happen? Do you want it to educate or generate inquiries or sell? Build your site around that. Your site visitor needs to be able to figure out your site goal in three to five seconds. The Home page of your website is the most critical, and not just to look pretty or be educational. Also, it's important to design a site that is interactive. Link to other pages. Give the visitor something specific to do. They might download an article, subscribe to your newsletter, or go on a virtual center tour. Also, keep it current. Get old dates off the site. Visitors will immediately leave if your site is out of date.

(*Author's note:* Prospects perceive that if you are neglecting your site, what else are you neglecting in your business?)

Julie: What specific elements of a website tend to cause visitors to stay on the site?

Anita: You want people to take action as soon as possible. They might view information or photos describing a specific program, look at a map of your location, subscribe to your newsletter, or contact you with specific questions. Put three to five bullets on the Home page with clickable text links. People tend to just scan your Home page. If they see something they like, they'll stay. If you want them to view a news article featuring your center, type the link in blue text and underline it, so they can click on it to go directly to that page.

Julie: What causes 'stickiness,' or draws visitors back to a site again and again?

Anita: The site has to change frequently. Change the copy, image, or quote on your home page each month. Have a section of "What's New." This could include a calendar, current activities or events,

latest press releases, statistics or trends for what's happening with child care services. Another way to get them back is to offer resources. This could be a brief description and links to a parenting tips blog, a review of recently-published children's books, or a map of your center in your geographical area. Make sure these links are pop-up windows, so your visitors automatically return to your site. Also, attempt to get reciprocal links so visitors from other related links can at least send an email request to you for further information.

Julie: How often should a website be updated?

Anita: At least quarterly remove old events, holiday hours, or anything that is outdated. Whenever you have new events or resources, update your site then notify current or potential customers of your new items. Encourage people to bookmark pages in your site and check back as they are updated frequently. On a regular basis, mark your calendar to review your website every quarter, add new photos, change text, and so on.

Julie: What traditional marketing activities should owners of early childhood education businesses do to direct prospects and customers to their website?

Anita: How many people are going to find out about your website off-the-web before they are online? Print your web address and email on every piece of paper and promotional material that leaves your office. Your web address and email address should be on business cards, brochures, letterhead, and envelopes. The recipients of these items will be prompted to take a look at your website. Maybe they have seen your site previously, but have not been back for a while, and will place your business card by their computer as a reminder to check it out. Postcards, labels, your center vehicle, Post-It® notes, and notecards are more places to put your web address.

(*Author's note:* I also recommend you add your website address to your email signature. Make it a hyperlink so recipients can link right to it. You can also add it to the end of your voicemail message with a phrase such as, "Meanwhile, please visit our website at . . . .")

Julie: What are ways centers can use their website as a business tool, in addition to an advertising and educational tool?

Anita: A great way to pre-qualify potential clients who visit your website is to add a *FAQ* or *Choosing The Best Care for Your Family* page. This will help fine-tune the types of prospects who will contact you about your center and services. To develop your own FAQ page, think of the top questions your ideal customers ask you. Browse your emails for the most commonly asked questions and your responses. When people are shopping for child care, either on or offline, the FAQ can help draw them to you.

Julie: What else is important in website marketing?

Heather: Have clear calls to action beyond *Contact Us*. Tell the visitor what you want them to do on that page, such as *Play Now* (for a video) or *Sign Up for our Newsletter*. Remember, your website can be a place to help you build a relationship with your prospects before they are ready to become your customers. The analogy I like to use is that you don't ask someone to marry you without dating them; users don't want to buy your services without trusting you are a good fit with what they need. So be obvious. Also, stay very focused with your site. Use solid keywords and good, action-oriented website design. Make sure you are proud of your website before you start driving people to the site through traditional marketing or social media marketing such as Twitter.

Anita: It's important to have a good working relationship with your web company. Ask what's new that may enhance your website. Technology is advancing as you are reading this article. Look at your website at least once a week and ask yourself, "What would improve it?" Check out your competitors' websites to see what they are doing and what you might do differently.

Julie: What are the best techniques for search engine optimization?

Heather: First, know how your customers search. Then be strategic. Pick one or two related keywords for each page. There is a free external keyword tool (https://adwords.google.com/select/KeywordTool External), which is a live database of Google searches by keyword. Pick keywords carefully and don't rush. SEO can be a six-month project before you break into first-page placement when you go organic (vs. PPC).

Anita: Use good keywords in your title bar, which may not be visible on your screen.

Keywords, meta tags, and meta descriptions need to be different on every page. These are behind-the-scenes, but will be found by the search engines. Your indexing should not be the same on all the pages of your site. Pick keywords that most define your business. Use words that your prospects will put in, such as child care, early childhood education, infant child care, or after-school program. Also include your geographical location. The top search engines today are Google, Bing, and Yahoo. While people are still surfing with their favorite search engine, there is a trend toward more online referrals. These referrals are coming from social media, well-written business blogs, and link exchanges with relevant, non-compete sites.

Julie: What are some tips on choosing good keywords?

Heather: There are three buckets of keywords. First are those entered into a search engine by the web surfer seeking information. This person might put in the word, 'childcare' or 'preschool.' Second are those words entered by people who are actively shopping. They might put in the words 'infant childcare.' Third are the words entered by the person who is ready to buy. This prospect might insert words such as 'accredited preschools in Larimer County.' You must know your target customer's path to purchase and select your keywords accordingly.

Anita: Use keyword phrases of two to five words. Many visitors will type as many as five words into search engines. Separate keyword phrases with commas.

Julie: How can center owners learn exactly what words their qualified prospects are using to search online?

Heather: The following site (www.spyfu.com) gives you a range of bids and how many times a specific keyword or phrase is being searched.

Julie: Where should keywords appear on a site to help the search engines find you?

Heather: Be clean and don't cross-contaminate your keywords. Assign words by page. Use a limited number of targeted, highly related keywords in title tags and distributed in page body copy. Visitors are using search engines for focused, targeted, relevant search engine results.

Anita: In addition to behind-the-scenes placement such as title bars, meta tags, and meta descriptions, the first paragraph of text is also crucial. Search engines pick you up based on keywords in your first paragraph.

Julie: What are your thoughts on Pay Per Click (PPC) versus organic methods of search engine optimization (SEO)?

Heather: PPC has gotten a bad rap. Why pay for visitors who search for a keyword phrase? Most people want a valuable search result without scrolling, and they decide in seconds whether or not they will select your site to visit. PPC can mean you are findable on page one. There is a competitive range of how much site owners are paying for a keyword phrase in a paid search. Google keywords start at a penny and go up. The more specific and targeted your keyword phrase, the fewer searches it will get, so it can cost less per search while giving you more qualified site visitors or those closer to buying. Do your homework before you commit to SEO.

Julie: What is the easiest way for non-technical owners and directors to check site statistics?

Anita: Sign up for Google Analytics. This is a free and accurate statistics tracking tool. Then ask your web company to install the script on your site. The script is not visible to anyone. The definitions of the terms are in Google Analytics, making it simple to understand the terminology. Unique Visitors, Page Views, and Referring Sites are the top three areas to review. Some web hosts also provide site statistics.

Heather: Google Analytics. By adding a small bit of HTML code to each page of your site, you can compare PPC and organic page search statistics. Site statistics can also give you an indication of whether or not your site is giving people what they expect to find. Most people will stay on a page no more than 30 seconds if they do not find something to hold them there.

Julie: How often do you recommend that child care business owners review their web statistics?

Heather: Monthly. The Google Analytics program walks you through important areas to review. If you have a high bounce rate on 80% of your site, it is time to redesign it.

Anita: I suggest you review your pages at least quarterly to see where your traffic is going on your site. If there is no action on a page you want to keep on your site, put something on that page to call visitors to action. You could add the option to view a video of your center's involvement in a special center or community event or a link to a white paper executive summary on brain-researched curriculum and its impact on kindergarten readiness. These add visual appeal to a static page. In addition, include some links that visitors can click on to go to other pages. Consider changing the name of that particular page; if it's currently named Curriculum, for example, change the page name to Learning at (Name of Your Company) or Virtual Tour of Classrooms or something that's more descriptive or intriguing to encourage people to click on that page.

Conclusion

Website marketing is an essential tool to add to your tool chest of marketing methods for your early care and education services. As part of a solid comprehensive marketing program, a unique, focused, compelling website can be a vehicle that draws your prospects and customers to you and helps them make the enrollment decision in your favor. Developing and maintaining a good website is an excellent way to make your marketing job easier. Make your website your marketing partner now so when potential enrolling families are driving the Internet highways to investigate, shop, and determine where to visit to make a selection, you and your center do not get left off the short list.

Resources

Visit or contact this article's featured experts:

- Anita Larson at The Web Muse & Co.:
  www.thewebmuse.com or
  info@thewebmuse.com

- Heather Lutze at Findability Group:
  www.findabilitygroup.com or
  hlutze@finabilitygroup.com.

Julie Wassom

Julie Wassom is president of The Julian Group, Inc., a training and consulting firm with a specialty in marketing and enrollment building in the early care and education industry. For nearly three decades, she has helped child care programs worldwide grow and reach a high level of financial performance. She is the author of the *Enrollment Building Success Library* of training programs and marketing tools, and the free monthly e-newsletter, *Wassom's Child Care Marketing Wisdom*. Visit Julie at www.JulieWassom.com.

Connect with Your Community

Reaching Your Program Goals through Social Media

by Kevin Carnes

It's easy to be skeptical about social media, isn't it? Posts, pins, likes, and tweets. What's it all for? But as it turns out, there is a very real point to social media. This is certainly the case for early learning programs trying to spread the word about their services, their involvement in the community, and their commitment to early childhood education.

I know from experience that most providers survive through word-of-mouth. One parent tells another about a great program, that parent tells another, and so on. But social media is word-of-mouth writ *very* large — and the potential benefits for quality child care programs are equally large.

Who uses social media? Although it's hard to believe, there are nearly 2 billion users worldwide[1] — and the numbers keep growing. Here in the United States, use of social media cuts across every demographic you can think of: income, ethnic background, urban setting, suburban setting, rural setting, age — you name it.[2] As a result, the opportunity to connect is truly unprecedented.

Photo by Lakeshore Learning Materials

Although using sites like Face-book, Twitter, and Instagram takes a little getting used to, these sites are wonderfully effective tools for promoting your program. And let's not be coy, they're cost-effective, too — because few things are as cost-effective as the word *free*. That's right! The majority of social media platforms are completely free for their users. In other words, there's nothing to lose, but much to gain, when these platforms are used to your advantage.

And there is no better time to get involved. Since so many high-quality programs are already using social media, some great resources are available to you. Reach out to these colleagues so you can discover what is working best for them:

■ Which platforms do they use most?

■ Which tools are most effective for reaching their supporters?

■ How much time do they spend on social media each week or each month?

Now let's talk about some of the concrete benefits of using social media!

Share Resources

Outreach to the Community

Celebrate Achievements

Inform Partners

Advocate for Children

Listening to Others

Share Resources

Social media platforms allow you to share information in all kinds of ways — and sharing resources can help you develop a following and keep it engaged. For instance, you can share at-home learning activities, summer STEM/STEAM projects for early learners, parenting articles, videos, and more. And by sharing these tools for free, you're opening the doors of your program to a much wider audience, including families and potential supporters from your community.

If you don't have the time to create your own content, you can share web links and other materials from respected partners. From local museums to nature centers to early childhood organizations, you can

Photo by Lakeshore Learning Materials

connect your followers to a variety of resources with the click of a few buttons.

Outreach to the Community

Along with sharing resources, other types of direct outreach include promoting events and special offers through the creation of event pages. From fundraisers to live performances to year-end 'graduation' ceremonies, what you share is up to you.

Social media also allows you to create unique hashtags to highlight specific events or topics of common interest. This provides your followers with a handy way to engage in public conversation about things that matter to them. Examples of hashtags might include: #HeadStartAnniversary, #WeLuvParentVolunteers, #MyChildCareFundraiser.

In addition to events, you can also promote practical things affecting the day-to-day operations of your program: everything from job openings and volunteer opportunities to simple schedule changes.

Celebrate Achievements

Use your social media presence to celebrate employees and program achievements. Recognize teachers of the month, good citizens, and more. Or, with a simple blog post, you can thank parent volunteers for all of their hard work — and give a special shout-out to generous donors. Plus, you can upload photos and videos to highlight success stories, certifications, and new accreditations. Every time you share an achievement, you're letting your families and followers — as well as advocates and politicians — know how engaged your program is with the community at large.

Inform Partners

In addition to keeping parents and families informed about special days and activities, social media allows you to communicate effectively with regional partners, early childhood organizations, and others. With just a tweet or an update, you can let sister programs in your area know about upcoming conferences, giveaways, teacher appreciation events, and much more.

Advocate for Children

Another great benefit of social media is the easy access it provides. If you want to share your concerns about an issue affecting the early childhood community, it's easy to raise awareness. A simple post or hashtag really gets conversations going — conversations that can lead to fundraising, lobbying, and working with others to find solutions.

Social media's distinct advantage over other types of communication is its ability to 'go viral.' Whether you're trying to get the word out to your community of followers or to the wider world, social media is the way to go.

Listening to Others

But social media isn't simply a megaphone. It's a two-way conversation. Using these different platforms and networks allows you to ask questions — and elicit feedback in meaningful ways. Social media sites even have tools to help you organize your communication and follow trending topics of conversation. For example, TweetDeck helps users of Twitter manage all of their posts, profiles, and pages.

This all sounds great, but I know what you're thinking: How will I have the time to do all of this? Well, setting up accounts with sites like Facebook, Twitter, Instagram, and Pinterest doesn't take much time at all — and you don't have to use any of their tools you don't want to use. And if you're all thumbs when it comes to the Internet, don't hesitate to ask a friend or colleague for a little assistance. (Hint! Local community colleges are also great resources — with students in computer science programs who are eager to apply their skills.)

So whether your program is large or small, home-based or center-based, social media can help you reach a wider audience, develop stronger ties to your community, and provide better services for your children and families. Do yourself a favor and get started!

A Word about Privacy

Privacy is a top concern for users of social media worldwide. To that end, many sites allow users to create public pages that anyone can view — as well as password-protected pages and services for members only. Like Kids & Company — Lakeshore's on-site preschool for employees' children — many child care providers opt for password-protected pages. Be sure to consider your options carefully as you create your own social media presence.

Always Remember to...

- post relevant topics such as *Week of the Young Child.*

- elicit responses with multiple-choice questions and fill-in-the-blanks.

- post weekly to keep engagement consistent and site ranking high.

- tag images and posts so users can link to partners and organizations.

- give 'shout-outs' to thank donors, parents, and volunteers.

- proofread for common errors and typos.

- get consent for use of photos of children.

References

1 Projected 1.96 billion for 2015 per Statista, Inc.

2 Pew Research Center

Kevin Carnes

After college and before joining Lakeshore in 1980, Kevin Carnes served as a VISTA volunteer, working closely with the Head Start community. There, he discovered the value of quality early education and knew he had found his calling. Before becoming President of Lakeshore's Education Division, Kevin served in many other roles in his 35 years with Lakeshore, helping the company expand from its humble beginnings in Northern California to a nationwide leader in education. He has served as a featured workshop presenter at NAEYC for nearly two decades and as a keynote speaker for national and state conferences all over the country, including NHSA, CAEYC, and many more. In 2008, Kevin helped Lakeshore forge a partnership with DonorsChoose.org, working to bring educational supplies to classrooms in need. That same year, Kevin was instrumental in making Lakeshore's on-site preschool part of the outdoor classroom movement, and soon the preschool — Kids & Company — became a certified Nature Explore® classroom. His work with the Arbor Day Foundation and the Dimensions Foundation helped earn Lakeshore the 2013 Rachel Carson Award for taking a leadership role in nurturing children's sense of wonder about the natural world.